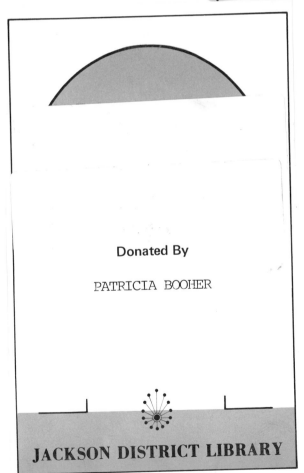

REFLECTIONS OF A WYOMING SHEPHERD ON THE
23rd Psalm

Patricia McClaflin Booher

authorHOUSE®

AuthorHouse™
1663 Liberty Drive, Suite 200
Bloomington, IN 47403
www.authorhouse.com
Phone: 1-800-839-8640

First published by AuthorHouse   3/17/2009

ISBN: 978-1-4389-6155-2 (e)
ISBN: 978-1-4389-5871-2 (sc)
ISBN: 978-1-4389-5872-9 (hc)

Printed in the United States of America
Bloomington, Indiana

This book is printed on acid-free paper.

Front cover image: Big Horn Mountain range, Photography donated by KL Reed, Shell Wyoming

WWW.PATRICIAMAC.COM

This book is dedicated to my grandchildren

Erik Steven Booher
John William Booher
Anna Marie Booher
Elizabeth Eileen Booher
Reagan Michael Booher
Kameron Elbert Musashi Lewis
Gabriel Josiah Isao Lewis
Perry Wallace Saburo Lewis
Luke Mitchell Ross
Maximus William Ross

And any future children in our family

"All your children shall be taught by the Lord,
And great shall be the peace of your children."
Isaiah 54:7

Acknowledgments

I consider it the highest honor to have the privilege of writing about this beloved 23rd Psalm, which is universal. Walking with this Shepherd of Heaven throughout my life has been a journey of faith and courage. These last few months of finding that quiet place to pen stories to the pages of this book have been a joy.

There are so many people that have cheered me on. I have listed just a few. For all of you that have come alongside me, I thank you.

One of the greatest pleasures to me has been enjoying all the seasons in the lives of my children. And then add to that the mates they have chosen; I feel doubly blessed. Each of them in his or her own way has cheered me on in the process of writing this book. They have patiently sat and let me read to them chapters and snippets of stories. At times when I would be so moved with raw emotion in penning to the page those stories with so much depth of feeling, they would just hug me for a bit as the tears would come. My son and his wife are Craig and Sandy Booher. My daughters and their husbands are Shana and Paul Lewis and Rachel and Mitch Ross.

This book is dedicated to the grandchildren and all future children to come. Each of them makes my life rich in creativity. They shower me with love and fill my life with joy and laughter. My eldest grandson is Eric Booher, and then comes John Booher, the twins, Anna Booher and Elizabeth Booher, and Reagan Booher. Shana and Paul's children are Kameron

Lewis, Gabriel Lewis, and Perry Lewis. Rachel and Mitch's children are Luke Ross and Maximus Ross.

My mother and father, Wallace and Edna Mae McClaflin, gave me the roots and fiber to write this story. It was the look of pride I would see on their faces that gave me the drive and stamina to finish college degrees that have served me well. Their bold faith to build a life on virgin soil on a homestead in the northern parts of Wyoming is a heritage rich with color, integrity, and a work ethic that has followed me throughout my life.

My brothers and their wives, hands down, have loved me unconditionally. They have been my cheerleaders throughout this journey of life. My elder brother and his wife are Mike and Linda McClaflin. My younger brother and his wife are Wayne and Pam McClaflin.

The Heart Mountain homestead community gave me a sense of place and belonging.

The passion and zeal that came alongside while writing this beloved 23rd Psalm were enhanced a great deal by the prayers of so many. The entire congregation has prayed for me through the entire process. I will mention just a few names of those persons that stood a prayer vigil daily for me: My children and grandchildren, Pam and Tim Sass, Virla Harrell, Cindy Thomas, Betty Sights, Mary Ellen Fraser, Georgia King, Ruth and Joe Shadler, Mom, and on and on it could go.

When it came to computer technology, my grandson Eric Booher and Robert Sight are nothing short of awesome. Their patience with me is commendable. This manuscript would not have been possible without both of them. Robert's abilities as a professional photographer have given me wings to fly in preparing those pictures chosen to depict the story of the 23rd Psalm. Dave Gazlay came along side and helped with editing of pictures, and for that I am most grateful.

Working with Authorhouse Publishing Company has been a pleasure as so many have assisted me. I want to acknowledge some professionals who have spent hours patiently walking me through the process of publishing. Jessica Young, Author Advocate, Megan Little, Sales Consultant, and my Editor whose encouraging words challenged me to bring the manuscript to completion, Joseph Fatton. Cassidy Taber, Publishing Manager, walked me through the final process and I am most grateful.

I have many forever friends but I will list some of those that have significantly made an impact on this manuscript. Ronnie and Teddy Jones gave of themselves so unselfishly, in their friendship and in allowing me to write their life stories as shepherds. Their knowledge and caring of the flocks of sheep they have been assigned is a beautiful picture in relating the 23rd Psalm. The many years Teddy and I worked with UW Extension gave a foundation for many of the stories found in this book.

Virla Harrell has the heart of an artist. Her dedication in transcribing the many interviews for the homestead project was a backdrop in putting together parts of this shepherd's story. Her painting of the Wyoming shepherd that went to Africa with the church mission team will be with those children of Kenya for a long time to come. Her many years of friendship are treasured by me.

KL and Linda Reed are my forever friends from Shell, Wyoming. The photographs they so willingly shared have made a great contribution to the story. The cover picture atop the Big Horn Mountain range will always be cherished.

Linda Bearup has been a forever friend for a good many years. I would describe her as my encourager. She gave me faith to stretch my wings and fly.

Joe and Ruth Shadler have been special friends for many years. They have encouraged me all along the way with this joy in writing I have been blessed with.

Mary Martin helped me take creativity to another level. Her friendship and the opportunities she gave me in attending "Quilting in the Tetons" were incredible.

Dr. Ben and Betty Silliman are special friends I have greatly appreciated. Dr. Silliman introduced me to resources in Family Resiliency that have been invaluable throughout my career.

Ray and Phyllis Sammons are just like family. Phyllis and I grew up together riding horses on the Hoff ranch. We will grow old together sharing stories and enjoying the grandchildren.

Dear Mary Ellen Fraser, what a special friend, who many times sat quietly while I read her stories from the manuscript. We have been friends for many years, and she is cherished.

Steve and Suzy Sammons have both been great encouragers as I have begun the process of publishing. I greatly appreciate their support and friendship.

Mary Beth Topa came alongside and edited the manuscript. Her insight and encouragement were timely, and I am so grateful to her.

Ann Blackwell transcribed and typed interviews in lightning speed with a smile. She has been an inspiration to me.

The years spent with UW Cooperative Extension Service were invaluable for me as I expanded and grew in so many ways. I am grateful for the doors of opportunity that were afforded me. As I read through the chapters of this manuscript, I want to give credit to four directors of UW Cooperative Extension who helped me immensely; they are Jim Debree, Darrell Kauztmann, Edna McBreen, and Glenn Whipple. Steve Aagaard, UW Extension Associate Director, encouraged me while working on the homestead research

I don't know if anyone has ever been more excited to receive their college diploma then I was. It was like a dream come true for me. I feel I must mention just a few of the many professors who invested so much into my life. Dr. Judy Williston and Dr. Phyllis Young expanded my horizons in Child Development. Dr. Elaine Found is a role model anyone would want to follow. Dr. Duane Laws gave me layers and layers of knowledge and insight I have relied upon. Dr. Betty Barber challenged the fiber of my foundation, and for that I am grateful.

And so the list could go on and on, but for those of you that quietly came along side, and have not been listed, my heart is full of gratitude to you also, as this manuscript is now coming to completion, a seed has been planted, and the season of it's fulfillment is before us.

CONTENTS

INTRODUCTION

The January winter had set in, and the Christmas holidays were but a memory now. The grandchildren's quilts had been completed just in time. I keep reminding myself I can't sew way into the night like I used to. But the children took delight in seeing the smiling faces of cartoon characters looking back at them from the quilting patches sewed with a great deal of love. All the sewing supplies and boxes of fabric had been taken back to the basement, and the New Year was upon us with all its expectations.

A team was evolving within our congregation in preparation for a mission trip to Kenya, East Africa, in June. The projects that would be a part of this trip would be to build a roof and foundation for a church in Kisumu. During the day and evenings we would conduct services along with a Children's Crusade.

From many past experiences of writing children's curriculum, I wanted to contribute to our mission team, so I asked if I could design the lessons that would be taught to the African children. As I prepared myself for this endeavor, something began to burn within me. I found myself returning time and again to the 23rd Psalm.

23rd Psalm

The Lord is my shepherd, I shall not be in want.
He makes me lie down in green pastures,
He leads me beside quiet waters,
He restores my soul.
He guides me in paths of righteousness
for his name's sake.
Even though I walk
through the valley of the shadow of death,
I will fear no evil, for you are with me;
your rod and your staff, they comfort me.

You prepare a table before me
in the presence of my enemies.
You anoint my head with oil;
my cup overflows.
Surely goodness and love will follow me
all the days of my life,
and I will dwell in the house of the Lord forever.

This particular Psalm is universal as it reaches across all denominations and beliefs. I had grown up loving the words of this chapter of the Bible. The impact on my life and the power in the words would forever be as a seal on my heart, after quoting it over and over just before a catastrophic car wreck in a snowstorm out in Shirley Basin in Wyoming in February of 2001, while traveling to the University of Wyoming (UW) for a conference.

I had been working on a qualitative research project entitled the "The Impact of Growing Up on a Wyoming Homestead." I spent several years interviewing three generations of homesteaders in the Heart Mountain community near Powell, Wyoming, where I had grown up. The research came to take on a life of its own, so in order to bring the project to a close, I applied for a sabbatical from the university.

Glenn Whipple, Director of UW Cooperative Extension, had called me in my Big Horn County office. I picked up the phone and said hello. Glen got right to the point: "Patty, I wanted to be the first one to tell you, we have just gotten word that you have been awarded a year sabbatical to do your research." I think I screamed in his ear. I was just beside myself; driving the car home was hard, as I felt like I was flying like an eagle.

Many of the original homesteaders had already passed away, so there was an urgency to complete the research so that the documentation and book could be completed. I hadn't planned on the project getting down so deep in my heart. The interviews that were taped and transcribed were with family members, friends, and neighbors who had taken a vital part in my own life growing up.

Trying to keep up with the responsibilities of work, along with conducting research that required a good deal of travel, was relentless. The project needed to be finalized, so with the anticipation of a sabbatical, I could see the light at the end of the tunnel.

It was a busy week before heading out that Sunday morning for the university, which was a seven-hour trip. Some Extension colleagues I would be seeing were close friends I had grown up with out on Heart Mountain homestead community. They had been my cheerleaders from the very beginnings of the research project.

Life can be full of surprises, and these unexpected experiences can change a person's life. I remember vividly quoting the 23rd Psalm and feeling a wonderful presence of God's love for me as I drove late in the afternoon on that bitter cold Sunday in February. I do not remember colliding with the snowplow. I can only recall the bone-chilling blast of wind that blew into my face as I looked into the scared, weather-worn face of a man I had never seen. I did not realize till later that his look of fear was because he was afraid I had been killed on impact.

I was so happy to be alive; I was not going to complain about anything, but recovery was a long process. I went into the sabbatical year slowly recovering, with my strength greatly depleted. My expectation was that the project would be completely done in a year. That was not going to happen. I kept working for the university, but the close call with eternity out in the middle of nowhere did not set well with my son Craig. He wanted his mother in Michigan, and he was not going to take no for an answer. Going through an experience like I did out in Shirley Basin helped me realize how quickly life can pass before us. With this realization, visiting grandchildren on holidays wasn't enough any more.

It took a great deal of soul searching but I came to the conclusion it was time for me to retire from my position with the university. I decided to completely change careers. I moved to Michigan and became a real-estate agent. The plan was that I would do this part time, and with the extra time I would write and spend time with all those grandchildren. I took on this new challenge with gusto. Learning quickly, I was immediately surprised at just what it meant to become a part of the real-estate business. Days melted into weeks. Months passed so quickly, and then several years.

After a time, I found myself waking up in the night with a heavy heart, knowing I had been given more time on this earth to complete the writing and research. I was perplexed because by the time I came home, many times late at night, I was too exhausted to write. Along with the exhaustion, my mind was so full of work-related tasks; there was no room to come away to that quiet place the writer has to find.

So this is where I found myself on a weekend on a frigid January morning in Michigan. Families wanted to stay nestled near the warm fireplace. Looking for a new home was not a first priority for clients. As was my custom, I was enjoying a strong cup of coffee, sitting on the couch with my little Yorkie-type dog, Timmy. I was saying my morning prayers and reading the Bible.

Thoughts began to surface. I turned to the 23rd Psalm. I read it over, line by line. I hurried upstairs to my office, turned on the computer, and began to write what was coming so rapidly to me. Childhood experiences with the lambs out in the sheep barn came back with intensity. And with the writing came a soulful weeping from the depths of me. What was I to do with this? I couldn't take on a new writing project now, as the homestead research was like a heavy weight on my shoulders.

I would wake up in the night, my mind full of thoughts of this Great Shepherd of Heaven, Jesus Christ. The drive within me could not be dismissed. That was the beginning of the story of a shepherd girl growing up in the northern plains of Wyoming. The simple, yet profound, life experiences of learning to know this loving and protective shepherd filled my thoughts. It only took a few weeks of writing to realize I had been gone too many years from the homestead to remember the day-to-day tasks of a shepherd caring for flocks of sheep.

Along my life journey I have been blessed with many friends who have loved me unconditionally. The names of just a few of my cherished friends will be entwined in the stories in this book.

My family has cheered me on throughout the process of writing this manuscript. I am sure at times they were a bit concerned, as the weariness was apparent. They have listened to my stories and given me a quiet space, and for that I am most grateful.

When I used to travel to Michigan for the holidays, I would sleep on the big couch in Craig's living room. Early in the morning my eldest grandson, Erik, would slip out of bed and come in and sit by me and read the most wonderful stories he had written. I was so taken by his gift of writing that I gave him a big thick thesaurus for his birthday. That has been several years past, and now he is a teenager. He plans to be a teacher, which thrills me, but he also has become very proficient on the computer. He has spent a good deal of time with me this summer helping me to acquire the skill of using a USB store-n-go memory drive. I am impressed that I can even tell you what it is. He was patient as he worked with me over and over, but the lessons he taught me have been invaluable, as it has helped me save many documents that could have easily been lost.

Virla Harrell came alongside me and transcribed all the taped interviews for the homestead project. She is a watercolor artist, so she has always wanted to see Heart Mountain for herself, as it would always come into the conversations with the homesteaders.

Teddy and Ronnie Jones have been lifelong friends. Our families were neighbors out on the Heart Mountain homestead community. Both families raised sheep. Teddy and I spent many years growing up together in the 4-H youth program, and we were the greatest of friends.

It was because of Teddy that I came back to Wyoming. She had told Jim Debree, former Director of the University of Wyoming Cooperative Extension, about me, and I was contacted out in Oregon where I lived at the time. My job application was accepted and I took a position as a Family Consumer Science Educator. Because I had grown up in a family so involved in 4-H, I once again came alongside the 4-H agents, assisting in the work of the 4-H program. Teddy and I worked together in a number of trainings and with the county and state fairs. So once again I had renewed a friendship that had begun in childhood.

The importance of these special people came into clear focus after the car wreck. A few months after the crash, while I was recuperating, the words came to me for a poem that has become my favorite. It is entitled "Forever Friend":

Forever Friend

Seasons come and go,
Spring, summer, fall, and winter,
A time for crying and time for laughing,
A time to be silent,
A time to speak.

In all of these seasons there is glue that runs down into the crevices
of the soul,
And upon the open wounded places of the heart.

This adhesive is what brings courage in the most trying of times,
Brings a smile upon a face masked in tears,
Hope is renewed because of this glue,
An ointment so valuable no price tag can be placed on its worth.

What is this glue you ask?
Let me tell you in a hushed tone of reverence.
This is my forever friend.
That one who believes in me when I am discouraged,
Who sees beyond today and helps me remember my dreams,
Forgives me when I don't deserve it,
Will cheer me on when I pursue the destiny and vision for my life,

Will grow old with me,
And we will remember the seasons fondly,
The tears, the laughter, the disappointments, and the triumphs.
The spring, the summer, the fall, and winter.
My forever friend and that is you.

Patricia, May 2001

The words of the poem are a picture of my forever friends. And now I find myself on another journey; writing the stories of taking care of bum lambs while a young girl out on the homestead. One evening after a long day of working, I went to my home computer and began writing the stories of my childhood experiences with the sheep. I pulled out references for information I needed. There was nothing to do, but go back and spend some time in the lambing barns.

I called Teddy and Ronnie Jones right during the lambing season, which usually began in the middle of January. I had job obligations so it wasn't possible for me to fly to Wyoming until March. Teddy was concerned, as the lambing season would be over by that time.

I contacted my mother, who still lives on the Heart Mountain homestead, and my brother Wayne and his wife Pam, who live on the McClaflin farm across the road. My enthusiasm for spending days in the sheep barns must have been contagious, for as I told Virla of my plans, she wanted to come along and finally get to see the mountain she had heard so much about, visible from the homestead.

I had many job obligations, so I worked feverishly to be able to take some days away, booked a flight, and met Virla at the Denver airport. We spent the day preparing for the drive to Wyoming the next morning. We were up at dawn and off we went across the prairies of Wyoming on Interstate 25. We drove up over the Big Horn Mountain range on Highway 14. As I was again seeing the beauty of the switchbacks on the western slope, I was in awe of my old stomping ground.

Our time was limited, but I just couldn't drive across Wyoming without driving down through Shell Canyon and stopping to see KL and Linda Reed. There really aren't words to express the beauty of the Big Horn Mountain range. The artist in Virla would have to see it for herself. We stopped at the cattle bridge, a place I had visited often while living in Shell. It was so good to see my dear friends. The minutes ticked by too quickly, and then we were off to see my family, waiting out on the homestead.

Homestead women know how to cook like no other, and Mom had a hearty meal ready for us. Wayne and Pam came over that first night, and excitement was in the air for this project that had been placed so deep inside my heart from a lifetime of knowing this Shepherd, described in the 23rd Psalm.

I had been calling Teddy every few days, hoping there would still be lambs being born when we arrived. The lambing season had come to a close. I was greatly disappointed, for as the time came closer to being out in sheep barns again, I wanted the thrill of watching a newborn lamb with its mother.

The next morning was a typical early March morning, cold and windy. In fact the winds could be classified in gale proportions. The clear cerulean sky overhead had winds that sounded like a freight train rumbling over the plains. It was unnerving as Virla, Mom, and I got out of the car. Here came Teddy with that wonderful smile, bucket in hand, out of the gate. Her hugs were always like a small mother bear's, and now I would be able to introduce two of my special forever friends.

The excitement was contagious; it was as if each of us shared a mission from on high. Teddy's face was radiant. "Patty, I have a surprise for you."

My heart pounded hard. "Oh Teddy, what is it?"

"We had a set of triplets born this morning!"

I wanted to run out to the barn right then, but Teddy needed to put part of the lunch in the oven. I went to the farmhouse with her, paced around the living room, wanting to get out in the barns. Ronnie had been called, as he had gone out early in the morning to begin plowing in preparation for spring planting.

And then we all went together, tape recorder in hand, out to the sheep sheds. There in the lambing pen, with fresh straw laid out, were three beautiful new lambs.

The mother was a beautiful Suffolk ewe with a black face. There were two black lambs and one white with black spots on his face. The spotted-faced lamb would be named Sammy, and he would be used as a narrator for the children's story.

This was an answer to prayer, for I had asked the Lord if it could be possible for a late lamb to be born while we were on the Jones farm. So God with his wonderful humor sent us three lambs, just hours before we arrived.

Ronnie came out to the barn, and we walked around taking pictures, and trying as best we could to glean wisdom from Teddy and Ronnie, who are shepherds with hearts that love the flocks of sheep that God has entrusted them with. Teddy introduced Virla and me to Nathan Splitstone; he is a shepherd who works at the Jones farm, helping with the many flocks. He was a great help to us with taking the pictures of the lambs. We liked his hat, as it looked like a well-worn large-brimmed design that spoke of many life stories.

At noon we went back to the house, and Teddy introduced Virla and me to a black Suffolk lamb and a white Columbia lamb. The black-faced lamb would be named Bo, and the white-faced lamb would be named Susie. While caring for the ewes and lambs, Ronnie had found Bo with an open sore. He didn't know what had happened, but he had brought the little lamb to the farmhouse for Teddy to nurse back to health.

Sometimes a ewe will not receive her lamb, and this was the case for Susie. Her mother had crushed her ribs and broken her back leg. Susie was also brought to the house and cared for with loving hands.

The work required to care for hundreds of sheep begins early in the morning, and sometimes can go throughout the night. The sheep sheds were a busy place, but also the farmhouse was filled with activity. Teddy would care for Susie and Bo throughout the day.

Farm women cook meals that are hardy, so Mom was in the kitchen often, helping Teddy preparing the next meal. That first morning after the feeding was done, Ronnie came into the house. We sat down at the dining room table, I sat up the tape recorder, and the interviews began. I went down through the 23rd Psalm, verse by verse. After a few minutes, I relaxed, asked very few questions, and listened to a shepherd with the heart of a pastor. After lunch was over, and Teddy was free to be interviewed, I was again taken with the nurturing heart of a woman who had a deep love for God.

When it was time to feed the bum lambs, I felt like I had come back home to my roots. Throughout the stories of the 23rd Psalm, I will share excerpts of the wisdom and description of the nature and life of sheep given by Teddy and Ronnie in our many conversations, which were taped.

The trip came to an end too quickly, and then it was time to drive back to Longmont, Colorado, where Virla lives with her husband, Gordy. It was early in the morning; we hugged Mom, Pam, and my tall, handsome brother Wayne; and we were off for the nine-hour drive across Wyoming. Virla got out her paints, and while I drove, she painted a picture of Ronnie holding the little lamb named Sammy. Neither of us realized, on that day, that the picture of a gentle Shepherd holding his lamb would make its way across continents to be in the hands of many African children in just a few months. As I flew home the next morning, there was an excitement, as to just where and what was happening with the stories that were coming from life experiences.

When I was back in my home office at the computer, the stories began to take form about Sammy, Bo, and Susie. Early on I realized these stories of the lambs would be going to Africa with the team. As I worked way into the nights, day after day, the pictures of African children would formulate in my mind. I will speak of this in the chapters to come as I tell of how the depth of life's richness was penned on the page in the next few weeks, and I was blessed.

This season of life, watching my grown children and enjoying grandchildren, is a blessed time. I realize my childhood growing up on a Wyoming homestead is rare in today's society. The wisdom I gained from the times I spent out on my horse Snip riding over hills and dales, seeing the massive Rocky Mountain ranges close by, has given a measure of richness to my life. Those times working along with my family out in the sheep barns and feeding bum lambs has given me treasured memories.

I can't remember when I began to love this Great Shepherd of Heaven, but I grew up with a sense that He walked very close to me, speaking to me on the wind, and in the quiet of the sheep barns. In my journey of life, I have found many other persons who have not had the privilege of knowing this Shepherd, Jesus Christ. The drive and passion that has brought this story of life lived on a homestead in northern Wyoming into focus is because I have come to love this Shepherd of Heaven so dearly. I think often of fellow travelers who have lost their way or maybe have never had the opportunity to know this kind and loving Shepherd from Heaven.

"My people have been lost sheep; their shepherds have led them astray and caused them to roam on the mountains. They wandered over mountain and hill and forgot their own resting place." Jeremiah 50:6

Teddy and Ronnie have lived out their life's calling in being Godly shepherds to the flocks of sheep entrusted to them. Throughout this tender story, I will share with you many life experiences of my own, as well as the wisdom of these shepherds who have been so kind to open their hearts to you.

Let me take your hand and let us journey together back into the lambing sheds and walk across newly plowed fields on a Wyoming homestead. May I have the privilege of introducing you to this Shepherd, described in the 23rd Psalm?

CHAPTER 1:

The Lord is my Shepherd, I shall not Want

When I was planning the short trip to Wyoming, I was grateful for the many experiences that had been afforded me during the many qualitative interviews I had conducted in regard to the Heart Mountain homestead project. During that research I was still working with the University of Wyoming, so I had many resources I could tap into, including professors who conducted this type of research. Rick Ewig, Director of UW American Heritage Center, had been a valuable colleague in the research project. I had read books on how to conduct qualitative research, as I felt a great desire to do the best I possibly could. The community where I conducted the research was where I had my roots, and I felt a great deal of commitment to those homesteaders. When I first began going into homes to conduct interviews, I would be anxious, but after a while I learned to relax. I had a checklist for myself and a supply bag with everything I could possibly need. There were specific questions I would ask each family, but after they had been answered, I would just sit back and let the family members tell their life story.

So now here I was again, about to interview family members and friends from childhood. Teddy and Ronnie Jones had both spent a lifetime on the farm. The day-to-day experiences with raising sheep had given them an understanding about life not often found in the urban society of today. This was not just a job. After walking through the barns and watching how they cared for their flocks of sheep, it was apparent that being a shepherd of flocks of sheep was a God-ordained appointment for this couple.

After the interviews had been transcribed, something became very apparent. As I read over the accounts of parts and pieces of the 23rd Psalm from the eyes of earthly shepherds, I was made aware of the wisdom and enlightenment of scripture that was conveyed by these fellow sojourners walking this path with God.

Wyoming shepherds, Teddy and Ronnie Jones
holding triplet, Sammy

Lamby Stories

I had returned home with a grateful heart, knowing the time with family and close friends had been like a breath of Heaven. There had been such a sacrifice of time and energy given to Virla and me in those few days on the old homestead. Now it was time for me to pen on page the stories that were formulating in my mind.

Those little lambs out in the sheep barns had gotten down into my heart. It was as if I had gone back to my roots as a child, caring for the lambs. I would check with Teddy every few days to see how Bo was recovering. One evening she had to tell me he had died. I couldn't believe it.

"What happened, Teddy?"

"I don't know; he seemed to be getting stronger, but I went to town, and when I came back he was lying on the mat next to the front door. I knew something was wrong because Susie was running all over the yard, crying, 'Baa baa,' and then running back to Bo."

When I got off the phone, I felt terrible. What was the matter with me? It was a sick little bum lamb It was a sick little bum lamb I would never see again anyway. But I was so disappointed. With the news of Bo dying, the faces of little African children were center focus in my thoughts as I would write. At times I was overcome with weeping; I would have to stop for a time and then begin writing again.

I would reflect on a time just a few years prior when I was out in the middle of badlands in Wyoming with brutal winds blowing into my car, which was crushed all around me. I had to wait for an hour for an ambulance to come and help me. I wasn't afraid, just bone-chilling cold. And now I was thinking about those little African children in desperate situations. Were they afraid, as many of them had already watched their parents die of terrible diseases? The Shepherd of Heaven would whisper to me in the night, "Take the 23rd Psalm to these children of mine across the oceans."

The day Virla and I drove back across Wyoming from spending time in the sheep barns; she was painting a picture of Ronnie out in the barnyard with the triplet Sammy in his arms. We decided the picture would be a shadow overlaid with the words of the 23rd Psalm. When we arrived in Longmont we went to see a graphic artist, David Nelson, who had worked with Virla on other projects. It took some time to describe what we had visualized, but we finally were happy with the outcome.

One Sunday morning as I drove to church, I stopped at a red light. It just came to me in an instant. It was a picture in my mind. It would take some investigation, but I was determined. I needed to locate the 23rd Psalm written in Swahili. Both the English and Swahili version would be placed as an overlay of the lamby picture with Ronnie.

My brother Mike and his wife Linda had been missionaries in Africa for twenty years. At present he is the Regional Area Director of all of Africa for the Assembly of God denomination. They now live stateside but both of them take many trips to countries all over Africa. Mike is one of my heroes, but then Linda is an incredible human being in her own right. She was the one who always had the gift for writing. The Lord has given her a special appointment. Across Africa, every year all the 400 Assembly of God missionary wives know they will receive a personal birthday card with a hand-written message from Linda.

I knew they would be the best source in finding the Swahili version for the 23rd Psalm. I was excited about the inlaid picture. When I told Linda we were going to pass them out to the children, she said, "Be careful, you will be mobbed with the children." I did not have a context for what she was telling me, but our mission team would soon find out.

The picture was sized down so four copies would fit on a page. Virla wanted to contribute to the mission's endeavor, so she had hundreds of copies made. A group of volunteers from our church helped to laminate the pictures. We cut them out with a hole at the top, and inserted yarn that would fit over a small child's head.

The final preparations for the mission trip were completed and the team was ready to head out. As each member pulled on their backpack, they were given a large plastic bag containing those little pictures of the Wyoming shepherd.

The mission team was met at the Nairobi International Airport by Debbie and David Barthalow. David was a building contractor from the States. He and Debbie had felt a divine call to go to Africa to oversee the building of churches. Before the week was over, every team member would not only love this couple, but would have the greatest respect for both of them, as the dedication they possess is an act of God's grace.

They took us to the mission compound to regroup, take showers, and get ready to head out to Kisumu. We drove by the home where my brother Mike's family had lived when I had visited them several times years before, when they were missionaries in Africa. Pastor Rachel had connected with her Uncle Mike so that our mission trip would coincide with one of his and Linda's many trips to Africa. It was with excitement and tears concealed that I saw them drive up. We had lunch with them and then they were off with a full schedule.

As we loaded up and headed south across the Rift Valley, I became anxious. What about these lamby stories? Would the children understand about sheep? And so my fretting along with jet lag came over me. As we drove along the highway looking down in the valley, the sights and sounds and aromas of Africa came back to me. I had many special memories of spending time with my brother's family from years past. As I looked out over the side of the road, I began to see sheep tied up so they could graze along the highway. That first morning when we were taken to the job site, what would I see, but herdsmen with flocks of sheep.

The Children's Crusade was to be conducted in the late afternoon, as the mission's team could not stay on the work site after dark, because of safety issues, and there were no exceptions.

The first night, after the lamby stories had been told and Pastor Rachel preached, we began to hand out the laminated picture of Sammy and the 23rd Psalm. By the second night, Linda's warning came to pass. Hundreds of children were mobbing the team handing out the pictures. One of the tall African pastors took the large bag, held it high above his head, and ran across the dirt road, the mobs of children running after him. It was such a funny sight; we laughed a great deal over it, at the same time realizing these children had nothing of material value. This little picture was a treasure to them. They would be thrilled during the day, as the men would give them the empty water bottles. This would become a toy they would play with all day. The little laminated picture could be seen hanging around their small necks.

By the third night, the team had gotten organized with the help of the African pastors. After service the children were lined up and we would go as quickly as possible down the lines, handing out the lamby picture. The Great Shepherd of Heaven finds all children precious in his sight, and he knew just what would bless them. Long after we had returned home, I am sure the children wore the inscription of the 23rd Psalm around their necks. I prayed often that it would be a reminder to them, that they were loved and the Lord could take fear out of the heart of the smallest child.

It was hard to leave the children every evening. There were so many of them crowding around us that I would just put my hand on their heads and bless them in Jesus' name. The vans would be loaded with darkness setting in. "Where is Mama Craig?" I would be out in the midst of the children. It is customary for mothers to be addressed with the name of the first born, so because Craig was my eldest child, I would be addressed as "Mama Craig."

Just two years later, there would be a terrible uprising in that area of Kenya, and some of the church members were brutally murdered. I have to trust that the little picture with the 23rd Psalm inscription was an avenue for the life-changing words of the Bible to find a resting place in the many children we quickly learned to love.

A great deal of thought went into the story about the lambs we encountered those few days in Wyoming with Teddy and Ronnie. The story that came out of the situations with the triplet named Sammy, who was used as the narrator, Susie the Columbia lamb, and Bo the Suffolk lamb, are not so different then one would find among persons we walk along with in everyday life. It was decided that there would be two books written about the 23rd Psalm. The story of the Wyoming shepherd and the orphan lambs would be a children's book. The adult version would be entitled "Reflections of a Wyoming Shepherd on the 23rd Psalm."

I couldn't decide what the title would be for the children's book. One morning while sitting in the quiet dawning of day, I remembered Teddy as she would go out to the barns and feed her bum lambs. With a big heavy bucket full of bottles of warm milk, she would call out, "Here, lamby, lamby, lamby."

"That's it!" Later that morning, I called Teddy. When I told her I had come up with a title, she wanted to hear it. "Well, Teddy, how does this sound? *"Here, Lamby, Lamby, Lamby."* I could almost see the smile break out on her face over the phone line.

The Lord is my Shepherd

When did I first meet the Great Shepherd from Heaven? I have had this question put to me many times. My first thoughts of God cannot be placed in a specific time frame, as I think I have had a realization of him from the time I was very small. Our family went to church, and I can remember Mom reading the Bible to Mike and me when we were preschoolers. She told of how she had received Christ when she was eighteen.

My grandmother Hannah Brown had a deep love for God, and I always felt very close to her. I didn't get to see her very often, but I connected with her, knowing I had a special place in her heart. Grandpa and

Grandma Brown lived in Gage, Oklahoma. When I was in the fifth grade, our family went to see them for the holidays. Grandpa Brown was very sick at the time and had to stay in bed. I always knew Mom loved him very dearly. Dad's sister lived in Forgan, so a few days after Christmas, Daddy took Mike and they drove to see his family. I stayed behind with Mom, as she wanted to spend more time with her parents. The day she said good-bye to her dad, my heart ached for her, as she felt this would be the last time she would see him. As we drove away, I somehow knew what she was feeling was true, and in March he passed away.

Our Heart Mountain community still did not have phone service, so very dear family friends, Bessie and Felix Hoff, were called. It was late at night when they drove out from Powell to give Mom the news. I was supposed to be asleep, but I lay quietly and listened to them. I heard Mom begin to cry, and with her weeping a great sense of loss came to me for a Grandpa's smile that we would never see again. She traveled to Oklahoma for the funeral, and while there, she had an encounter with God that would change the destiny of our family.

A few days later when I came home on the school bus, I was so happy as I walked into the house and saw Mom standing in the kitchen. As soon as I saw her, I sensed something different about her. "What has happened to you, Mom?"

She took me back to her bedroom and sat me down on the bed. As she began to tell me what happened to her, I began to cry. During her few days in Oklahoma, the Shepherd of Heaven spoke to Mom's heart in such a powerful way, her walk with God took on a new meaning. I had been praying for some time to be closer to God, and as she spoke, God answered my prayers. I asked Christ to come into my heart and become my Savior on that day, and I have loved him from that day on. I think I have always loved God, but on that afternoon sitting next to my mother, in a state of grief over the loss of her father, the Great Shepherd became my Savior.

The 23rd Psalm begins with the first verse, "The Lord is my shepherd." The word "my" describes a shepherd who loves each of us in a personal way. It was as if a warm and bright light was turned on in my soul that day, and prayer became very important in my life. I looked forward to the times that I could ride my horse out in the hills, and on those days I was very aware of God's presence all around me.

In those months after Grandpa passed away, we attended a small Assembly of God church. There was an altar that stretched across the front of the sanctuary. After Sunday evenings I would go up to the front of the church and kneel down by my pastor's wife, Sister Thiemann. The experiences I had during those times as a young girl at the altar have given me a foundation of God's love for me in a personal way that has given me the faith and determination to walk with God all of my life.

I certainly am not perfect. As the years pass, I realize more and more how much I need God's strength moment by moment. Throughout my life, when I have made mistakes and sinned, my heart has been so broken, because I discover as I take a diverging path, I do not feel as close to God, so I have always turned around and run back into his arms.

It is amazing to think that this same God who spoke from a burning bush to Moses, and gave songs to the shepherd boy David while out tending flocks, would come and love a little shepherd girl out in the lambing sheds of Wyoming.

Throughout the Bible, sheep have been used as a metaphor for the nature of man. As I look over the list in the animal kingdom, I can't help but wish we humans could have gone to a little higher rung on the ladder of intelligence and self-preservation. But alas, I will have to say from experiences out in the sheep barns with bum lambs and out in the pasture with stubborn old ewes, I do see some similarities to those of us who consider ourselves human.

The good news for each of us is that finding this Shepherd is the most wonderful experience anyone could have. If one were to ask a person who has spent a lifetime walking with this God of Heaven, the response would undoubtedly be similar to mine.

Some of the special pleasures in writing this manuscript were the interviews with Teddy and Ronnie. Throughout the chapters you, the reader, will also recognize the deep-felt passion of these followers of Christ.

Teddy's Introduction to the Heavenly Shepherd

I think one of the great thrills of life is to watch those special friends from childhood as they enter into this experience of knowing the Heavenly Shepherd in a personal way. As I sat across from Teddy listening to her, I was blessed.

Teddy began her story. "My walk with Christ had a long time coming. I'm like Moses; I was forty years probably in the desert. Yet way down deep, as I went through life, I realized that the thing that was so weak and lacking in my life was my spiritual side. I knew that something had to be done. Like so many people, I didn't have the time or the energy to devote to God and what needed to be done or how to do it. Yet I knew that someday when I had more time and energy that was an area I needed to really address and to work on.

"In my mind and down deep, I always knew that God was there for me and yet I was not willing to give back to God or let Him control my life. Then it all happened. God has interesting ways of working. I had worked as a UW 4-H Extension Agent for about twenty-seven years. A major change came to my life during a county fair time when things were not going well. I received a phone call and God spoke to me. I think it was just like a light bulb turned on; it was time for me to shift gears and to do something else. I went and talked to my husband Ronnie about retiring. I knew it was time I turned in my retirement and marched on. And as I did, I knew down very deep in my heart that I was to grow spiritually and start walking with God. And that is what I did. I got into a tremendous Bible study that turned my life around. I learned to read the Bible daily. I have learned to take God's Word and apply it to my life. I have a heartfelt commitment to being a servant of God so that I can bring God honor and glory. I have found a contentment that is beyond understanding, and with that comes much joy. He has blessed me with all that plus all my friends. I can just look back over my career, and I can see God's hand and how He protected me and how He guided me and how He blessed me without me even knowing it and was so patient with me. Now I hope that I can be His servant and give back for those many years that He cared for me and loved me. I hope I can bring Him the honor and glory of being His servant."

Teddy and Ronnie have spent a lifetime caring for sheep, but it has been many years since I have had that privilege. Many techniques of feeding are much more scientific then when I was a child, but oh so many memories have surfaced as I have once again returned to my roots.

Bum Lambs

My first recollection of bum lambs and how they have affected my life began to unfold as I would be teaching an adult Sunday school class in the Detroit area in the early eighties. It seemed the city would go on forever. There were times I would break away from a hectic schedule and drive for endless miles to find myself finally out in the country, just hoping I could see a sheep somewhere out in the pasture. Would I ever be out on the farm again, as the memory of another time came to mind?

Our three children were pushing on to the mark of their teen years. I had gone back to college to finish a degree in secondary education. Days were filled with many things, and there wasn't much time for personal reflection, as I strived to meet the demands of life.

It was a large adult Sunday school class. I didn't know all the students well, but I recognized all their faces. I guess I would describe myself as a down-home type, living life many times very practically with what my growing-up years would describe as having a lot of horse sense.

Regardless of the Bible topic, the stories would come to me, standing there in front of people who were very dear to my heart. There was a storehouse of memories from childhood tucked away from years of taking care of bum lambs, better recognized to readers as orphan lambs.

I would spend a great deal of time in preparation, but as the lesson would begin, the passion from within me would surface. The surprise to me was, not so much the women in the audience, but the men. These were not wimpy men, but hard-working fellows who thrived in the Michigan winter elements. When I taught, I would always seek for eye contact. I now call them my lamby stories, but in those days as my childhood experiences out in the sheep shed came up from inside me, men throughout the audience would be moved to tears. This was a surprise to me, thinking everyone had some semblance of what I had taken for granted all my life; those stories tucked away in my back pocket.

As life unravels at one's feet, the divergent paths along the way sometimes are a great surprise, and many times the path is down through some fairly deep valleys. I would never have dreamed that my greatest passion in life would be writing. But here I am now with a gentle peace in my soul, recalling the lambs from so long ago.

As I look back over my personal journey with this Shepherd of Heaven, there are some pivotal points that I know, without a doubt, his hand of protection covered my life. I can recall such a day out in Shirley Basin, while I was still working with the university.

Car wreck in Shirley Basin

I drove away from home that morning with relief, as I saw the sun filtering down through the clouds. I was hoping the rays of amber, layered with a soft mist of pink cotton candy softness, were a promise of a warmer day then it had been in this northern Wyoming country in early February. I was in for a brutal surprise that would forever change my destiny and with this, a passion for life that would ever drive me on.

I was an Extension Educator with the University of Wyoming. My office was housed in the county courthouse in Big Horn County, in the town of Basin, right at the base of the massive and rugged Rocky Mountains. I lived in the small hamlet of Shell, and from the picture windows in my living room I could see right into the canyon, a wonderful place to live for someone like me who loved the beauty of nature.

The university was in Laramie, which was approximately a seven-hour drive from my home. Traveling was an ongoing part of my job, as I found myself many times all over the state doing programs. Because I was so used to long trips, I had pondered for days why I had such an unsettled feeling. I had called my mother several days before, asking her to pray for me, as I couldn't shake this uneasiness. I had a habit of rising early to watch the sunrise coming up over the mountains, as I didn't want to miss the splendor of such beauty.

The Sunday morning I was to leave, I was up at five, long before I would see the first gray glimpse of dawn. As I sat in my chair, with my gaze fixed on the eastern skies, sadness came over me. Although it wasn't an option, I just wished that I could stay home. Finally around seven, I finished loading my bags in the car and returned to lock the front door. This wasn't a usual custom, but on that morning, I opened the door, looked around to my familiar things, and said, "Good-bye, little home." I started my Toyota Camry and headed down the hill and began my long trek to Laramie. On my many journeys, there was a familiar awareness that angels would accompany me. I would pray that the Lord would send angels to travel along with me, and this morning was no different.

As I drove through the town of Basin, I realized I had to get hold of this melancholy mood, or it was going to be a very long day. I reached into my stash of recordings and pulled out a tape of sermons from my daughter Shana, who lived in Seattle. On a regular basis, she would send me tapes of her pastor, Reverend Steve Schell of Northwest Foursquare Church. The topic was on praying many kinds of prayers. I popped it into the cassette player. The words he spoke were like healing salve to my emotions as I drove down the highway. By the time the tape had completed, my mood had been elevated into a tranquil state, and it relieved me as I calculated I had clipped off an hour of my journey as I drove down into Thermopolis. Driving through Wind River Canyon regardless of season was a scenic pleasure. It was always a relief to see Shoeshone lying out there in the horizon, as it was the halfway point. For as long as I could remember, this stop-off place was like the very end of somewhere.

I cruised through the small town, and headed to Casper. For the next two hours, I sang old hymns. There have been times in my life that it seemed as if Christ was sitting in the seat right next to me; this was one of those days. The melancholy mood had melted into a feeling of strength and peace, as the songs brought so many memories of a lifetime of experience.

Just a week before, I had received word that I had been awarded a year sabbatical to complete a qualitative research project. I was still so excited about the news, and it was going to be wonderful to have time to share my gratitude with friends who had been such a support through all the hard work of accomplishing the task of writing.

Much planning had gone into this week, as close friends I had grown up with, who also worked in Extension, would be attending the week-long training. We had arranged to have adjoining rooms at the motel. Each of us had stashed junk food into coolers. This had been the arrangement on previous trips, which had proved to be disastrous to anyone staying in the rooms adjacent to ours. We were the greatest of friends, and as the week would become tiresome, the evenings would grow in warmth and much laughter, as old stories were rehashed. I had always been blessed with an overactive sense of humor, so my retelling of past adventures would take on new and colorful dimensions. And of course, being the true-blue friends that they were, they would laugh at my antics.

By the time I had left Casper, it was the middle of the afternoon. The constant wind that customarily engulfs this area was unusually strong. Since the sun was still shining, I did not realize, as I drove along, that the temperature had plummeted. As I looked back to the Medicine Bow Mountain range to the northeast, I saw dark volumes of seething, angry clouds coming down upon Shirley Basin. This was an area surrounded by a mountain that created its own climate. I had remembered my mother commenting in the past, "You don't want to get caught in Shirley Basin when a storm comes up."

Now, my mother was one of those homestead pioneers, who took on a form of bravery, not common to the modern-day woman. Her words had resonated in my storehouse of memory, and for that reason, if I had to drive through Shirley Basin in the winter, I was always relieved to see the sign, "Medicine Bow, 22 miles."

My Toyota Camry began to pull to the side of the road, and I quickly realized the wind had risen to gale proportions. I slowed down and gripped the steering wheel, trying to hold the car in my lane of traffic. Loneliness seemed to engulf my thoughts, which became a companion with those feelings of foreboding that had left home with me. I began to recite the 23rd Psalm over and over. I had just finished the last verse, "And I will live with you forever and forever and forever." Suddenly, I cried, "Dear God, send me more angels."

As I came down a hill, my car must have hit a patch of black ice, along with wind gusts, which caused the vehicle to begin a spin that went around and around in huge circles into the oncoming lane. Of course, there were no cars in sight, but as I spun around the second time, screaming the name of Jesus over and over, terror struck my heart as I saw, coming out of snow flurries, a huge snowplow coming directly towards me.

I was amazed, as I believed I was going to see God at that very moment. Thoughts passed so quickly, and there was an awareness of how close I felt His presence all through the day. It felt like a dark force had pushed me from behind right to the side of the huge plow. Then the darkness came.

Someone was banging on my window. I was gasping for air, as the blasts of wind were brutal on my face. I looked up to see a look of panic on the face of a man I did not know. The winter elements of wind and cold had caused deep wind-burned wrinkles, but he had a look of kindness. I would later feel sorry for the driver of the snowplow, as he thought I was dead. My car was on the side of the road, with a lone hubcap from the front wheel lying in the middle of the pavement. The snowplow was parked across the highway, the side of the bed smashed and the snow blade bent up into the air. I felt disoriented, and all I could think was for him to call my brother Wayne, who lived on a farm near Powell.

The highway patrolmen quickly arrived. He brought me a small quilt to wrap around my legs. It would take an hour for the ambulance to arrive. As I sat there, with most of the windows shattered, I realized the car was crunched in all around me. My seat was broken; glass was everywhere. I looked down and noticed my stomach had begun to swell. I lifted my shirt, and the entire front of me was purple. Panic seized me for a moment, as I knew I was hurt. Would I freeze or bleed to death out here, so far away from my family? Instantly as the thought came, I saw my son's face with such a depth of sorrow in his eyes. My father's memory came to me so clear, as if he was right there in the car. I took great strength from the last words my father spoke to me, before his death from the ravages of cancer: "I'll never give up hope, I'll never give up hope."

I quickly assessed my situation and came to the conclusion, "I am not dying today, I'm not cold, and I'm not going to cry. I am going to be thankful for that kind man over there sitting in the cab of the snowplow and the poor fellow out there having to wave the traffic around the debris my car left in the road."

I later was told the temperature had plummeted to more than twenty below. I just wanted to go home, but that was not going to happen, as the roads were closed behind me.

When the ambulance arrived, five volunteers had come to help. By this time, the sun had gone down, and the cold and wind currents had dropped again. The front passenger door had been shoved almost to the middle, so I was relieved they got the door open. A man got in and lifted me up out of my seat as the others managed to get me out from the driver's side. When the full impact of the wind blast hit me, I cried out, but then became immediately sick. The gurney felt like stone and it was hard to lie back, and the last thing I wanted was to throw up, knowing I probably had some broken ribs. I kept requesting blankets, as I couldn't ever remember a time in my life I had been so cold. I was so grateful for the many people who helped me that night, but I had an ache in my heart, as I wanted my family.

How many times throughout my life have I discovered the caring of God in some of life's small details, which can mean a great deal. My UW

Director, Glenn Whipple, came to the emergency room, which meant so much to me. To my amazement, the local pastor of the Assembly of God, who just happened to be my childhood Sunday school teacher, Dave Garrett, and his wife Jean came and stood by my bed until I had stabilized. I noticed that Dave's arm was in a sling. He had just come through a horrific car accident himself. I knew he was in a great deal of pain, but it was such a relief to me that they had come.

That cold February day seems but a memory to me now. There is one thing everyone who comes so close to death can agree on: You are forever changed as you realize you have been given more time on this earth. From my time as a very young child growing up out on the northern plains of Wyoming, I had an awareness of God as my loving Heavenly Father and Great Shepherd. Is it any wonder that the stories of me as a little shepherd girl would surface and would come to me with such intensity that I would have to pen them to these pages? I knew the voice of the Shepherd, and I could trust him, as he gave me the courage that day out in Shirley Basin. I invite you to come with me now, as I share with you my experiences of life walking with this wonderful Shepherd of humanity.

After the cold winter day out in Shirley Basin, I was warm again, and life went on, but it was never the same. I slowly recovered, worked hard during my sabbatical year, and spent another year with the University of Wyoming. My eldest was a son by the name of Craig. For many years, he wanted me to come back to Michigan, not just for visits, but to live. Finally one day, in the early morning watching the sunrise, I knew I needed to be near those grandchildren, telling them lamby stories, and investing in them on a regular basis. The decision was not easily made, but much soul searching went into this process.

Teddy and Ronnie Jones came alongside me in the moving process, which always seems to be more difficult then we want to acknowledge. We drove across Interstate 80, with an auto transport in tow. I sat in the front with Ronnie with my little Yorkie dog Timmy. Teddy sat in the back seat, holding onto their sheep dog with a heavy hand. He was a very smart dog, but he made me nervous, as the look in his eye suggested he had thoughts of the tasty morsel sitting in the front with shaggy ears.

Craig, Sandy his wife, my daughter Rachel, her husband Mitch, and all the grandchildren met us with open arms that cool and crisp day in late October. I was hoping there would still be some golden, vibrant red leaves holding on for my friends from Wyoming. So it was with great delight, as we came around the south edge of Lake Michigan, my Wyoming friends were greeted with smashing bright crimson leaves. Life is a trade off. Wyoming has the rugged mountains that will always be a part of me. And then we have Michigan, with its lush foliage with so many types of trees and lakes, I will never acquire all their proper names.

CHAPTER 2:

Green Pastures

As I read over the interview with Ronnie, transcribed from that special trip to Wyoming, I was struck with his insight and how much he sounded like a pastor. I would say he is a man of few words, but it was apparent he had spent a good deal of time thinking over what he would say to me. As I sat there that day going over each verse of the 23rd Psalm, I asked Ronnie about feeding sheep and how the food is digested.

"Sheep have three stomachs. The first stomach is where the sheep eats her food, which is usually roughage but it can be grain. The food goes into the first stomach and then the sheep rests peacefully. While resting, the sheep rechews the food it has eaten. This helps with digestion. After the food has been rechewed, it passes into the second stomach. The sheep will spend a good deal of time resting and chewing, which is termed chewing their cud. This is the second time the food has been chewed. The sheep looks peaceful and then will chew, chew, and chew. After a while this food is swallowed, the sheep will belch some more food, and the chewing process will begin again. The sheep is at peace when she is chewing her cud."

"When sheep are at peace and are not hungry, they are content. Psalm 23 says that sheep will lie down in green pastures. Sheep lie down and rest, especially during the long part of the day. They like to rest and chew their cud."

"Now if they have had dry feed that doesn't give them a lot of nutrition, they are not going to be at peace. The flock is going to move a lot more because they are looking for food. As a good shepherd, we need to bring them to lush green pastures so that they can be at peace and have plenty to eat and not have to roam so far to get what they want."

One of the most precious gifts that was given to Mike, Wayne, and me as we grew up was the love of nature. Our parents loved life on the homestead, but the special bonus was being surrounded on all sides by the great and mighty Rocky Mountains. Even after studying a topographical map, it is hard to fathom just how vast the wilderness areas are on the mountain ranges. As I reflect over the words spoken by Ronnie, a true shepherd of sheep, I recount the many times I would stand gazing out over high mountain pasture lands with bands of sheep in sight. Without the influence of Billy Woodruff, I wonder if our family would have become involved in the raising of sheep.

He had bands of sheep that would be transported every summer up into the highlands of northern Wyoming wilderness. Some of the bands of sheep were taken for summer pasture to the lower hills of Heart Mountain just west of the homesteads. We would see Billy driving up the road on a regular basis. I remember the first time I met Billy. He stopped one afternoon with a bum lamb. He asked mom if our family would be interested in taking on some bum lambs. Every few days another lamb was added to our little flock. Mom would feed the bums during the day, and then Mike and I got the early and late shifts.

At times when our family could get away for a few hours of fishing we would see the sheepherders with the wagons out on the mountain side as they cared for the bands of sheep. The life of the shepherds caring for these many hundreds of sheep was one of solitude. They lived in small sheep wagons, which would be moved from place to place as the sheep required new and fresh pasture lands.

Heart Mountain which can be seen to the west of the McClaflin homestead, Powell, Wyoming

Billy Woodruff

After spending the day in the sheep sheds with Ronnie and Teddy, Virla and I went back to the homestead with Mom. I wanted her to reflect on some of her many memories in those early years of homesteading, so we got out the tape recorder and began. One of the highlights for our family was when we went with Billy Woodruff on a fishing trip, so I wanted Mom to tell the story.

"Billy invited us many times to go with him up into the Beartooth Mountain range, up high where his sheep were taken for summer pasture. Finally one year Wallace said, "Okay, we're going to take three days and go." I remember the kids were so excited.

"Before we left, I asked Billy if he wanted me to take some lemonade. He looked at me like I was nuts. It was primitive up in the mountains, and we just drank water, as there was nothing fancy about that trip."

Sheep wagon in Shell, Wyoming, picture donated by KL Reed

"So off we went way up into the Beartooth Mountain range next to lakes where there were no roads. We slept in his sheep wagons and would ride on horseback before dawn to the most wonderful fishing spots. Patty can still remember eating those trout with the red fins and how delicious they were. In the evening, we would come into camp and the men would get a big fire going and fry up the fish with fried potatoes. In the morning, Billy fixed sourdough pancakes with bacon and eggs. In the evening, after supper, we would sit around the campfire and Billy would tell us some of the most outlandish stories about the early years in Wyoming."

"When Billy caught his first fish, he cut off the red fin, and that is what we used for bait. Everyone caught fish. We would ride horses way back to deep blue mountain lakes along deer paths. It was high in the mountains, so the sun rays were intense. We would begin at four in the morning to load up and ride for a long distance. We would be tired at night, but we all enjoyed being with Billy so much."

"Afterward we were so glad that we just decided to go because that winter he found out he had cancer, and passed away. I believe he was eighty-one. Such a nice fellow; we missed him so much, as we always had enjoyed the times he would stop by the house for a cup of coffee or a meal."

I am grateful I have my mother's voice on tape, and the words she spoke in transcript form. The trip to the Beartooth Mountains with Billy Woodruff is a highlight in our family's collection of memories. I can still remember the fun of catching the brookies in those icy cold mountain streams. Years later, after I was an adult and would come home to the homestead, Dad would be up at sunrise, down at Alkali Creek, catching fresh trout. By the time my family was getting up for the day, he was frying up the fish. He would sit back and enjoy watching me, as with great delight, I would enjoy my favorite kind of breakfast. But I think even to this day, the most delicious trout I ever ate was sitting around the campfire with Billy, listening to his scary stories.

I have had the privilege of knowing earthly shepherds who have been faithful to care for their flocks of sheep; how much more does the Great Shepherd care for the individual sheep in the form of you and me? Two portions of scripture that I read on a regular basis are chapters 37 and 51 of the Psalms:

> *"Trust in the Lord and do good; dwell in the land,*
> *and enjoy safe pasture.*
> *Delight yourself in the Lord and he will give you*
> *the desires of your heart." Psalm 37:3 & 4*

> *"Create in me a pure heart, O God, and renew a steadfast spirit*
> *within me. Do not cast me from your presence or take*
> *your Holy Spirit from me. Restore to me the*
> *joy of your salvation and grant me a willing spirit,*
> *to sustain me." Psalm 51:10 & 12*

It is God's desire that all of mankind would be fed in pastures of His righteousness and goodness. We have been given a free will to choose this life of rich abundance. The reason I have such a love for these passages of scripture is because of my own personal experiences throughout my own life, when I would ask this Shepherd of Heaven to keep my heart tender and pliable in his hands.

As each individual walks his or her personal journey through this life, heartache and trouble will come alongside at some point. The verse in Hebrews 13:5 says, "*Never will I leave you; never will I forsake you.*" This is vital to you and me in the times we are living. The personal commitment of taking the time to walk in spiritual pastures comes back to sustain us in the hard times. Having the insight to know that we have been cared for through the hardships by this faithful God is what brings the joy and peace so that we do find ourselves desiring to worship and praise the God of this universe.

I could pen many scriptures related to the Great Shepherd's desire to provide green pastures for his sheep, but I will settle for two:

> "*Then we your people, the sheep of your pasture,*
> *will praise you forever;*
> *from generation to generation we will recount your praise.*"
> Psalm 79:13

> "*Come, let us bow down in worship, let us kneel before the*
> *Lord our Maker; for he is our God and we are the people of his*
> *pasture, the flock under his care.*" Psalm 95:6 & 7

It says that the very hairs of our head are numbered. How God loves the deepest part of man, where he is not even aware, is beyond my comprehension. When I interviewed Teddy about how she fed and cared for the lambs, she spoke from a lifetime of knowledge and dedication to that calling she and Ronnie have given their lives for. I can pen the words from the transcript of Teddy's interview, but the emotion and compassion she possessed as she spoke could only be experienced in its entirety sitting there at the dining room table on that blustery March afternoon.

Shepherd's care of bum lambs

"You asked me to talk about one of my very favorite topics, and that is raising bum lambs. The more I am around sheep, it is apparent to me that this is one of my callings from God: to be a shepherdess and care for his kids, his creatures. It is so rewarding to take those baby lambs when their mamas don't want them and love them and care for them and watch them grow. God has created all those creatures, and so it brings me great pleasure."

"We start off our baby lambs, usually called bum, but you can call them an orphan. In the sheep world, we usually call them bum lambs. They are actually an orphan lamb because the mother cannot feed the lamb. We have two types of lambs we call bums. One group of lambs is fed a supplement, as the mother ewe will not have enough milk because she has triplets or one side of the udder is no longer functioning, so we have to supplement milk for the lamb. These lambs usually stay with their mother. The first nineteen days, these lambs will be fed three times a day, or twice a day, depending upon how much they are getting from their mother. We watch them closely to see how they are doing and judge accordingly. These lambs are fed until they are about forty-seven days of age. By this time the lamb can consume enough roughage in order to maintain and grow and really gain and do well. Before that time, their stomach isn't large enough to consume enough calories and nutrients."

"The other set of bum lambs are true orphans. They are taken from their mother for some reason. Sometimes we have a ewe that does not like her baby and so consequently she will be very mean with the lamb. If we leave the baby with her, she will butt it and could break the lamb's ribs. We have had to rescue some lambs with broken legs, such as Susie that we will tell you about. We had one ewe that lay on her lambs. We thought we had put too much straw in the pen, so we gave her another lamb, and she laid on that lamb too. She just didn't like the baby lambs at all, so she is no longer on the Jones farm."

"Sometimes a ewe will die and we will try and work that lamb onto another ewe. In four or five days she usually takes the lamb, but if she butts the lamb around we have to take it, and it will become a bum lamb. Some years we have an abundance of triplets, and because of space at least one of those lambs will become a bum."

"In the first two days, I have to make sure that the bums without any of the mother's milk are getting colostrum. We get this colostrum milk from the dairy. This first milk from the ewe or from the dairy is really important. If these lambs don't get enough colostrum they will look like they are doing well and all of a sudden they will get sick and die."

"We have documented this so we have learned through the years how vital the colostrum is in those first few days. It starts forming the antibodies that help to defend and fight off the diseases that the lamb might get. So the first two days I feed the bum lambs colostrum three times a day. After that, I mix the colostrum half-and-half with lamb replacement milk. A ewe's milk is high in fat content versus calf milk replacement, so it is important that we use the lamb replacement."

Teddy Jones feeding bum lambs on wooden feeder

"When I have a lot of bum lambs, I use a wooden board with eight holes for the milk bottles. I try to group the lambs by age and size. We feed each lamb ten ounces of milk per feeding. For the first nineteen days, we feed the bum lambs three times a day. This would be around the clock, as they are very much like a newborn baby."

"In each lamb pen is a feeder with lamb pellets that contain about nineteen percent protein. It is dense in vitamins and minerals to give the lambs a good start. It is very important to keep fresh water in the pens for the lambs all the time."

"We keep the lambs in groups of eight, as they can get around the feeders easily. They start forming friendships. Sheep are social animals, and if you take one of the lambs out, it will cry and cry because you have separated it from its friends. After we have moved the lambs from these small pens, we keep the groups of eight together because they have bonded to each other. Sheep are creatures of habit, and they like to be in familiar surroundings."

"After the nineteenth to the twenty-third day, we observe the lambs closely. This is the period of time when they start to consume a good deal of dry feed, and we are trying to drop back from the thirty ounces of milk a day to twenty. During this time is when the lambs will bloat, as the proportions of milk and feed are not balanced in the lamb. We give the lambs bloat guard starting around the tenth day, but we still have to watch them closely. Bloating causes gas to build up in the lamb's stomach. The stomach will blow up like a balloon and it can get so full, that the gas will rupture the diaphragm. The lamb will not be able to breathe, and it will die. This can happen in a matter of just a few hours. That is why it is so critical to watch these lambs very closely."

"If we can discover the bloating early, we will give the lamb milk of magnesia. If this doesn't relieve the pressure, the last resort is to stick the lamb's stomach with a long needle to release the pressure of the gas so it won't build up any more. This is a problem we have to deal with, as we can lose a lamb very quickly."

"Another problem we have with baby lambs is pneumonia. The bums suck fast on the bottle, and the milk can go down into the lamb's windpipe. If they can't cough up the milk, it will go down into their lungs and cause them to have chronic pneumonia."

"The third thing we have to be careful of is scours. This type of diarrhea in the lamb will cause it to become dehydrated very quickly and die. These are the three main killers of our bum lambs, so we watch them very carefully."

"As you can see from this very brief description, these bum lambs require a great deal of work and close observation. It is rewarding because they are just like children. They are your babies, and you know without your care they would end up in the trash can."

"We call them our trash can babies. If we didn't care for them, love them, feed them, and doctor them, that is where they would end up."

"It is rewarding, because these little bum lambs become bonded to their caregiver. They know your voice. When you go out and call, 'Here, lamby, lamby, lamby,' they just come running. Even after they become grown ewes, and have their baby lambs, they are not afraid. They will come right up and nuzzle you. They know who you are. Ronnie says, 'You've got to love them. If you don't love them, then don't raise sheep. Sheep can lie down and die so easily, so they need to be cared for and loved."

Once again as I read the description Teddy spoke of in her interview, there were pictures in my mind, so clearly remembered, of not only what she said, but how she truly loved those little bum lambs. How it brings to mind the Heavenly Shepherd, who desires to care for each of us in such a tender way. It is His desire to feed us with Heavenly manna. Each of us was in His mind, before this world was created. How sad that we often do not take the time to allow Him to feed us with spiritual food that will make us strong and at peace.

Our society has become very aware of the need for good nutrition, healthy diet, need for organic foods, and so on. The statement, "You are what you eat," has a good deal of research data to back it up.

I remember a song I used to sing in Sunday school when I was a young child. It related to the farmer sowing seed. After all these years, I think about the parable of the sower planting seed, and check my mind and heart on a regular basis:

*"A farmer went out to sow his seed. As he was scattering the seed, some fell along the path; it was trampled on, and the birds of the air ate it up. Some fell on rocks, and when it came up, the plants withered because they had no moisture. Other seed fell among thorns, which grew up with it and choked the plants. Still other seed fell on good soil. It came up and yielded a crop, a hundred times more than was sown." **Luke 8:5–8***

We are admonished to read the Bible. It is God's inspired word. I do not understand how it can be so life changing to make it a regular habit to read and study the Bible. I have found time and again, that at just the moment I need an answer or hope in a situation, those verses that are in my mind and spirit will come into clear focus like a road map.

Another source of inspiration is to read about saints who have gone before us. Many of them lived through crucibles of life's hardships, yet God was faithful to care for them, and this brings me courage. To realize that Jesus Christ loves each of us in such a unique and precious way fills my life with much joy.

CHAPTER 3:

HE LEADS ME BY QUIET WATERS

Three of my grandsons are approaching kindergarten. Reagan and Perry have older siblings, so the anticipation of the schoolroom is a high priority for them. Luke is the eldest of two, so going to school is a new concept for him. February is birthday month for Luke and Perry. I managed to find backpacks with their favorite cartoon characters. Perry got "Lightning McQueen," and Luke received his favorite, "Thomas the Tank Engine." The backpacks can only ensure that they will thrive in this growing-up world of school. We have "Grandma Preschool" on Friday mornings, but that is a far cry from what the real world has in store for these young men.

I will have to say their knowledge of the color wheel is very impressive. They can identify colors such as fuchsia, purple plum, cobalt blue, and pink sparkle with a smile. The large pasteboard castle that has been painted out on the grass with many layers of tempera paint is magnificent to say the least.

Shana and Paul had moved from Seattle with their three sons several years ago. Kameron the eldest has a mind for math, likes things orderly, and likes to beat Grandma in Dominoes. Gabriel is his mother come back in the form of boy, as he looks like her, and has a love of beauty. Now Perry is just Perry. He likes to carry around a blanket that is completely in rags and he has a charming personality. He and his cousin Luke like to look for dragons with fiery green eyes with Grandma in her attic and in the basement back room.

Grandsons painting: Reagan Booher, Luke Ross,
Maximus Ross, and Perry Lewis

The big blue tub

It was the middle of August, and all of us adults were wondering, where did the summer go? As all of our family members were watching the summer days quickly counting down, thoughts turned to the western shore.

The whole family thinks Lake Michigan is a special spot on this earth. In the spring, plans were made to spend many days in the sun, swimming in her waters. Hectic schedules and writing books come at a price, and it is called time. One late summer day my daughter Shana and I stopped the merry-go-round and decided we would take her three sons to the lake for the day. As we rushed around on that Friday morning, getting those last-minute items such as fresh bread from the bakery, the minutes ticked away. And then we were off; the sun was shining; the three grandsons had smiles on their faces; and we couldn't believe we had pulled it off.

The last time we had gone to Lake Michigan, we had discovered Van Buren State Park. It had been an overcast day; the water was as calm as a glass tabletop. The water was warm, so we swam for hours. I wanted to remember that special day, so I had the grandsons help me find unusual rocks I wanted to put in my flower garden at home. When it came time to drag the sack of rocks to the faraway parking lot, I did hear a few grumbles.

This time, I planned well in advance. I found a big blue tub at the Dollar General Store. It even had rope handles. Someone else must collect rocks, I said to myself. As everyone loaded into my van, heading out for a day at the beach, I came out of the garage with the big tub, travel cart, and bungee cord. No reply from the boys, but I did see a certain look pass over Shana's face, but in an instant it was gone. I announced I had brought this along to carry supplies down to the beach, but as she remembered last year's episode with the rocks, she had me figured out.

We took a different route on this trip, through farmland. Being a farmer at heart, I took delight in seeing all the rich soil, covered with an abundant harvest of fruit and vegetables. We managed to drive right to the park, and the excitement in all of us mounted as we wanted to head to the beach. We loaded up all our gear, food, towels, sunscreen, purple plum floating mat, half-empty very large blue tub with rope handles, and we were off to the beach.

As I walked along with a brisk step, pulling my tub on the traveling cart with big wheels, I felt very smug, and exclaimed, "Wasn't this a great idea?!" The same fleeting look passed over Shana's face as she replied, "Yeah, what a great idea, Mom."

As we reached the crest of the hill, the kids shouted, "Oh, look at the waves!" The sky was a cobalt blue, a perfect day in the sun. On the last trip to this beach, it had been almost deserted, but today all up and down for a good long way were other families enjoying the last days of summer before school began.

As I passed by the wooden post with the hazard sign for high waves, I should have paid closer attention. We found a perfect spot, dropped off the big blue tub, and were ready for a day at the beach. The waves were high so I waited on the shore, already excited about the beautiful rocks that would be my treasure-trove from this day with my family.

Shana and the kids headed for the waves. She had found a sandbar a distance out. I could see her as the waves would turn her over. Her exuberant laughter at the fun of the challenging waves was like music to my ears. Seeing the smiles and hearing the laughter of grandchildren at the beach has to be one of life's most special pleasures.

Grandma Patty with grandsons:
Gabriel Lewis, Perry Lewis, and Kameron Lewis

It was my turn to enjoy the waves. The grandsons exclaimed in unison, "Oh Grandma, are you coming in?" The water was colder this time. I inched out to about waist deep. A big wave caught me; off came my plastic flip-flop-type shoes; upended, I went down to the bottom, trying to right myself. The waves came again with a smashing force. This wasn't fun. I gulped and took in the lake water. The lake floor was covered with rocks. My feet are very tender, so it was hard to stand up. As I spit up water and called for the kids to grab my shoes, I looked over to see a couple standing nearby, watching this little old grandma. By the looks on their faces, I realized they thought I was in trouble. I sheepishly dragged myself out of the water as the boys ran and collected my shoes.

What happened to this lover of the sea? Seasons of life have a way of changing us. There was no way I was going to complain and put a damper on the exuberant laughter of my family. I realized I needed more substantial shoes if I was to tangle again with the waves, so I found myself very content as I walked along the wet sand at the edge of the waves on shore. For the rest of the day, I counted the heads of all four members of my family like an eagle on her perch, like a watchman on the tower, so to speak.

As we raise our children, the love we have for them is overwhelming at times. But when we grow into the grand parenting years, the love takes on a quality of seasoning from a lifetime of loving and experience. It will be a day full of memories for each of us, as we shared the love of that great expanse of lakefront together.

As I kept an eye on the waves and the four heads bobbing up and down as they swam, I looked for beautiful and exquisitely marked rocks. At first I laid the rocks in front of the blue tub, and then the boys wanted to help me look. I wasn't going to disappoint Gab, as he is an artist type such as myself, when he came back with a very large amber rock. "Well, that probably is too large," I said, but then after they all went back in the water, I slipped it under the towels. We didn't want the day to end, as it was so grand, but the hours of chasing waves had left Shana with an increasing case of sunburn and exhaustion. With great resignation, we had to announce it was time to go. The boys ran back for one more rigorous jump into the waves and then we packed up.

I had planned ahead when I tucked in an extra-heavy-duty garbage bag for the rocks. It was some distance through heavy sand before we would reach the walkway, which would allow the enlarged tires an opportunity to share the weight of those rocks. Kam was assigned to carry the plum purple-colored mat, and Gab would pull the plastic sack. Now mind you, not all of the rocks were in the plastic garbage bag. Some of those lovely specimens were still hidden in the bottom of the tub. Shana was in pain; the sunburn was kicking in. I really didn't want her to have to help me, but actually I couldn't pull the tub through the sand by myself.

Shana has inherited my sense of humor and can laugh easily at life's special moments, but as we turned around to see Gab in the distance, pulling on the bag with a touch of drama, I laughed uproariously, but she was serious. With a pained expression on her face, she addressed the issue at hand: "Kameron, go help your brother!" Shana went on to the van to get clothes for Perry, but Kam and Gab had to remain with me as they pulled the garbage sack. I went into the restroom to change clothes. I had taken the big blue tub into the small compartment in the restroom, fearful someone would steal the rocks. I couldn't have been in there for more than three minutes.

When I came out, I looked over on the sidewalk. The huge, dark brown garbage sack was covering the width of the walkway. Rocks were strewn across the sidewalk. Oh dear, I hope someone doesn't fall over the rocks.

"Kam, what happened?"

He stood over by a light pole, disgust written all over his face. "The garbage sack got a big hole in it, Grandma!"

I had no choice; I had to go over, pick up the ruined garbage sack, and try in the most inconspicuous way possible, to pick up the rocks and put them in my homemade hauler of heavy things.

By now, the evening heat was setting in. I began the long haul alone back to the van, as my family had all deserted me by now. No complaints from me, as I huffed and puffed along, amazed at how heavy those rocks had become. Shana and the boys were standing by the driver's side of the van. I pulled the cart around to the other side, pulled the sliding door open, and began unloading. I quickly took some of the rocks out of the carrier and laid them on the floor before hoisting up the tub, relieved that I could actually lift the tub and do the little task all by myself.

At last, we were all ready to go, exhausted, but so grateful at the wonderful day we had all experienced. The boys settled in for a long snooze, we hoped; Shana tried to get comfortable; and I drove along with dreams and visions of just where those lovely rocks would be placed in my flower garden.

I refer to myself as a "lover of the sea." My first recollection of fascination with ocean waves was when our family lived in Southern California before moving to Wyoming to live on the homestead in 1950. I was a preschooler at the time. My parents took us to San Diego to visit my mother's cousin Imogene and her family. They lived a few blocks from the ocean shore. I had to be watched carefully, as I would run without abandon right out into the waves. From that point on, I had a fascination for the ocean. The sand, the saltwater taste, the smells of ocean breezes, the call of seagulls all enfolded me into a world of fantasy and joy.

I go along for a spell and then for some reason, it is as if the ocean calls me to its shores and I have a deep longing to look out over the waves and smell the sea. If I were asked where I wanted to live, near my children and grandchildren would be the first call, but just behind would be a toss-up between the Pacific coastal shores of Oregon and the great Rocky Mountain range in Wyoming.

Cannon Beach, Oregon, has to be one of the most beautiful places on this earth, in my estimation. A few years ago, I spent six weeks there in a small bungalow. I had a view of the ocean at my window as I spent the daylight hours writing my homestead manuscript. It was the middle of October, so the evenings were cool. Every evening I would walk down to the beach with Timmy, my Yorkie-type dog. I would wear an old hat, sleeveless shirt, and walking shorts. I liked to run along right at the break of the water in the wet sand. Timmy would run off chasing seagulls, never with a chance of catching them. By the time I would be out of breath, my lips would be blue and my feet would be icy cold. It wasn't long before I was having some respiratory problems and a low-grade fever. I was so mesmerized with the beauty of the sun setting over the water, that only later would I reflect on others walking along the seashore as well. They were dressed with warm jackets, hats, and rubber knee boots.

The days grew too short during that brief period of enjoying the sea. Poems were written describing the deep-felt sadness of leaving that northern seashore.

BEACHCOMBER

Here they come one by one, some in twos, once in a while a group
of three talking and enjoying each other in this brief weekend
excursion to the beach.
I quietly walk here on the water's edge with my small Yorkie;
his small legs running, smiling as he goes. He loves the sand, but
seems to have an innate respect for the ocean waves.
We beachcombers have an instinctive respect for one another.
This ocean coastline is the solace place,
the spiritual sanctuary for the tired weary soul in a world of high tech,
daily demands, and global pursuits.

I know in my heart, my time here on this vast ocean sand,
walking barefoot,
with the crashing waves always the focal point in view, will come
to an end too shortly.
And so I have moments of grief of my departure, even now.
How long have I carried this dream of setting on the warm sand,
breathing in the
brisk morning air, filled with mist,
and smelling the soul-cleansing fragrance of salt water?
Passerby, you walk so quietly there.
Are you locked away also with your
creative inner thoughts of a rejuvenated spirit and soul?
Lovers in the distance, you walk together hand in hand.
Some of you so young, others walking with a cane,
helping each other in your slow and stumbling gate.
Are you seizing the moment, letting bygones pass away into the
vast ocean's expanse,
loving each other, cherishing the moments that will soon be gone?
I turn away giving you the privacy you deserve.
Walking on I pause, standing very still a few moments
watching the magnificent white waves
of foam silhouetted against turquoise water,
at the base of royal blue sky that reaches up into eternity.
Kindred spirit of the sea walking there so quietly, my heart blesses
you as you step so lightly, allowing my tears to come uninterrupted
as the inner voice within me is so overwhelmed by the thoughts
and phrases coming so rapidly,
I at times would seem to be swept into the depths of sorrow,
and then rapidly be thrust up into the greatest exaltation of soul.
I soon will take pen in hand and write, but for a time of reprieve,
I will again begin my stroll
along the beach with other lovers of the sea.

Patricia, September 28, 2000

When viewing the Pacific Ocean at low tide on a calm day, it is hard to fathom that this same body of water was where one of the deadliest natural disasters occurred in December of 2004. The tsunami that struck eleven countries with 100-foot waves in less than ten minutes was responsible for over 225,000 deaths. The human suffering from this natural disaster cannot be measured. Many people saw family members swept away by the mighty waves, and there was nothing they could do to save them.

The beauty and comfort of water, whether it be on a mountain stream or ocean coast, has been a focal point for many persons, as they will build homes right out on the sand, or near the falling stream over craggy rocks. Always in the back of the minds of individuals is the reality that this small body of water could become a flood of huge proportion with the right amount of snow runoff in the high mountains. The smooth and placid ocean shore has the possibility of turning into a catastrophic hurricane. This has been one of those summers when we have witnessed the destruction of many hurricanes. The nation is just realizing in small proportion the magnitude of Hurricane Ike. There was a mandatory evacuation up and down the seacoast, and yet many thought they could ride out the storm.

Life has its times of pleasure, peace, and much joy, and then are those times that it seems a flood has come and wiped away every dream and voice of laughter to be heard.

When my oldest grandson, Erik, was five and John was three, they came with their father to meet me in Buffalo, New York, where I had been attending the Creative Problem-Solving Institute. It had been an incredible experience for me to have the opportunity of spending a week at this conference, but also exhausting. The training was over, everyone was departing, and I sat waiting for Craig, anxious that he would be able to find me. The whole family had planned to come, but Sandy had to stay home with Elizabeth, as she had gotten sick in the night. When I saw him coming up the walk carrying Anna, with two young boys in tow, I wanted to cry with joy; it was so good to see my broad-shouldered son with a stocky build. We loaded up the children and headed off to Niagara Falls.

We first went to view the lower falls, which were nothing short of spectacular. What resonates in my mind as I bring that memory back into focus were the upper falls. Anna was in a stroller, and I had both boys' hands clutched firmly in mine. As we approached the upper falls, the water was flowing smoothly before it crested over the top of boulders. The power of the water was so great; it seemed as if we were standing on top of the current as it moved quickly by. We were protected by a security fence, but just the thought of one of my grandchildren falling in those fast-moving waters brought a dread to my mind.

If it were possible to sit at a safe point and watch the tsunami that swept across the Pacific Ocean, one would have some grasp of the mighty power water can have. Or if there was a platform one could stand on right in front of the waters of the Niagara before she makes her mighty plunge downward, holding out hands with palms up to push back the volume of water, could we understand the power of this magnificent waterfall?

Not only is water a thing of power that can bring great destruction, but it is vital to human existence. The human frame can go much longer without food than water. Dehydration is a word I respect, after an experience I once had. I found myself being rushed to a hospital in Cebu, Philippines, after a long night of sickness. Before that morning, I had never realized how quickly one could become so dangerously ill in such a short time. I recovered but the experience left me weakened for a period of time.

I always get uncomfortable when watching a movie where the actors are lost out in a desert, all water is gone, and they are disoriented as to where the water hole is. I want to get up and go get a drink of water.

During my teens, one of the summer excursions every year was to take a group of 4-H friends up to the top of Heart Mountain, which looked to the west of our farming community. About ten of us of would load up in the back of the pick-up truck, and my brother Mike would be the driver. I am relieved as I watch my grown children being so careful to strap their children into car seats today. I shudder when I think of some of our trips up the mountains in those teen years back in the fifties.

On one such trip, each of us was carrying part of the picnic that was to be eaten at the base of the rocky ledge at the top. This was no small climb on that hot summer day in August. I don't remember who was to blame, but the person carrying the water jug dropped it on a big rock and broke it. This was early on, so we climbed most of the way without water. When we finally got to the top, we sat down under a tree for shade and tried to eat the sandwiches. They were hard to choke down. Why I remember the frosting, I haven't a clue, but someone had brought an angel food cake with orange frosting. As I looked at it, I was reminded of the hot sun up above. We didn't want to be rude, so we all ate a piece. It was a hot, grumpy group of teenagers that came down off of Heart Mountain that afternoon.

Many years have passed, and I trust I am a bit wiser. When I drive through the parkways, with all of the running paths, I see young people all equipped with their thermoses attached to belts. There is an awareness of the need for a constant supply of water.

My parents were fishermen, so if Daddy had a pause in irrigation, we would head up to the North Fork to fish in the evening. It was not uncommon to drink out of a creek or dip a metal cup down into the river. One always hoped that a dead animal was not lying in the creek around the hillside, out of sight.

Life has changed, as the concern of water contamination is something to be contended with. Bottled water has become a common commodity in homes today. How I would have enjoyed a bottle of water stuck in my back pocket the day I ate the angel food cake with orange frosting.

I lived in Shell during most of the time I worked with UW Extension Service. During that time, there was a seven-year drought. The Extension Agriculture Agent worked closely with ranchers and farmers, and also my family was farming in the Powell area, so the seven-year drought was something I was very aware of. It was sad to drive through Wyoming and see it dry up. After a few years, because of such a shortage of water, crops were plowed up, or not even planted. Summer ranges were diminished for summer grazing. In an arid land like Wyoming, it would be foolish to waste water. The land where my home was situated had water rights. I was always very careful when I watered my trees that I used only what was needed. Later in the summer, the water supply would run out, which became difficult for everyone living in that area. Water is vital for survival.

The importance of still waters and green pastures is contained in verse 2 of the 23rd Psalm. Teddy and Ronnie both expressed the need for nutritious food, as well as a steady supply of fresh water.

I asked Ronnie to explain the significance of the portion of the verse, "Leads me by still waters."

He replied, "Sheep require a considerable amount of water to help out with digestion and with body temperature regulation. Still water gives the sheep a better chance to get a good drink. It is more difficult for sheep when the water is fast moving. It is more peaceful for them to go up and get a drink if the water isn't splashing in their face. Sheep don't like to have water thrown in their face, just like you or I wouldn't want water splashed in our face."

"Sheep also have a sense that they don't want to get down in the water, as it drags them down. When the wool gets wet it becomes very heavy, so it can be a danger to get up and out of the water."

During those days we spent in the lambing sheds, Nathan would be making his rounds on a regular time schedule, checking all the pens to ensure the sheep had a steady supply of fresh water.

In a spiritual sense, Jesus speaks of thirst and living water in relation to God's spirit dwelling within man.

> *"'If anyone is thirsty, let him come to me and drink.*
> *Whoever believes in me, as the Scripture has said, streams*
> *of living water will flow from within him.'" John 7:37*

Each of the gospels relates the incident when Jesus had been ministering to the throngs of people; evening was setting in and he was weary. It was time to go to another location. He and the disciples got into a boat and headed across a great expanse of water. In his weariness, Jesus went to the stern of the boat and fell into a deep sleep. A furious squall developed and waves were about to sink the boat. The disciples were terrified that they would drown.

> *"The disciples woke him and said to him, 'Teacher, don't you care if we drown?'*
> *He got up, rebuked the wind, and said to the waves, 'Quiet! Be*
> *still!' Then the wind died down and it was completely calm. He*
> *said to his disciples, 'Why are you so afraid? Do you still have no*
> *faith?'" Mark 4:38–40*

The Shepherd of Heaven walks closely, and yet there is a responsibility for each individual to have the discipline to feed on green pastures of

God's goodness. Also to allow the Spirit of God to run as a fresh stream through one's life, as described in scripture; it will sustain us when the difficult times come. I am reminded of the verse:

> *"When the enemy shall come in like a flood, the Spirit of the Lord will lift up a standard against him."* Isaiah 59:19 NKJV

How many times have these words spoken in Isaiah brought me new courage to keep on this journey I have been on since a young child, like sands of the sea, I cannot count them.

CHAPTER 4:

HE RESTORES MY SOUL

A short phrase found in the context of one of most well-loved chapters in the Bible, the 23rd Psalm, "He restores my soul," has resonated meaning to countless individuals down through the ages.

The society we live into today wants a quick fix for the melancholy that comes with heartache and loss. One would only need thumb through a magazine off the shelf, and glance at advertisements for just about any kind of product. Do we see downcast faces, agonizing over losses? Hardly; smiles and greetings of the good life full of bliss, with no cares for tomorrow, greet us, page after page.

The real picture of life does have those days that we could describe as downcast. The Psalmist David gives us a picture of the sadness and the distress that follows: "Why so disturbed within me?" This was not a constant condition for David, as the verses preceding this lamenting question describe him as going with the multitude into the house of God with joy and praise. And in the second part of this verse, we see that David had discovered how to handle his times of discouragement and how his strength would be renewed:

"Put your hope in God, for I will yet praise him, my Savior and my God." Psalm 42:5

Looking back over a time in my life that seems but a long-ago memory in many ways, there was a pivotal point in my own personal destiny. Our family had come through a tragedy, which had affected each of us. The grief I felt was relentless, as it seemed one wave of crying would be met with another. And then there were times I couldn't cry. During those days I poured myself into my work, driving myself to the point of exhaustion. The human frame does not thrive under this kind of pressure. I found myself being rushed to a hospital to be operated on for a ruptured disk in my lower back. The surgeon had reassured me that I would be just like new. What he failed to mention was that I would not be able to work for months and the pain after surgery would be worse than before.

I called my brother Mike and asked if I could borrow a recliner chair that was in his trailer parked out in the back yard of Mom's home. I wasn't going to be able to sit up in a chair for some time. He, of course, said, "Yes." I stayed with my mother for a few days after surgery, but the mountain range in view just outside my living room window was like a healing balm I needed to recover, so a friend loaded up the chair and took me home to Shell. I lived very simply, could not drive, but as I lay in the recliner looking out at the clouds up over the mountain horizon, holding my little dog in my lap, the Shepherd of Heaven came very close alongside, giving me hope that would soon turn into a surprise that I would never have expected.

*Shell Canyon seen coming down the west side of Big Horn
Mountain range in Wyoming*

After my children were raised, I returned to Wyoming, the place of my childhood. I took a position with the University of Wyoming Cooperative Extension Service. The county where I was placed was near the Big Horn Mountains. I found a lovely home at the base of Shell Canyon. From the picture windows and wraparound deck of my home, I had a breathtaking, panoramic view of the lower mountains. I made a point of watching the eastern horizon over the tops of the purple mountains for the sunrises in the morning, and would finish the evening watching the radiant sunsets to the west.

Birth of a writer

The day that is vivid in my mind is the day I began to write. I had been alone at home for several weeks recovering from the back surgery. It was a cold day in March, with heavy snow falling all day. I could not sit up, so I was lying in the recliner, looking out over the distance, studying the jagged outlines of rocks of the mountain landscape being covered with a blanket of snow. My heart was sad, and I was feeling overwhelmed with pain. As I sat there, I was swept with an urgency to write. This was a surprise to me, as writing had always been difficult. I managed to get out of the recliner and go find a tablet. As I lay back down, I took a pen in hand and thus began a new chapter in my life. I wrote one page after another and would then read what I had actually put down.

I wrote one poem after another. Those first writings have been tucked away in a safe place. To have the courage to be able to pen those sorrows buried so deep inside was the beginning of inner healing for me. I put dates on each poem, later being very thankful, as I could see by the content, as time passed, my writing began to change. I came to an awareness that in the melancholy times I could draw strength and reflection that would be translated on the pages as hope and faith for the future. Those were not wasted days, as I recognized a sharper keenness to my surroundings, and insight into the suffering of others.

My own story can be described as a mirror reflection of others who find themselves in life's tragedies and call out to the Great Shepherd. How God takes the hard places and turns them around to build character in the heart of man is a constant reminder to me of His majesty and greatness.

At this point in my journey, when people ask me my view of life, I say with a chuckle, "I am going to be happy if it kills me." I was born with a laugh that seems to consume me and draw others in as well. For a period of time, I didn't laugh very much. As I reflect back on the harder times of my own life, I find it interesting, those words that others spoke to me, that gave me the determination of a bulldog, to grow, regardless of the situation.

I would fly back to Michigan for the holidays, usually finishing up a quilt or French heirloom dresses for the grandaughters. My children always had a list of their favorite foods they remembered from childhood. I suppose this shows my homestead roots. When my own children were growing up, I wanted them to have vivid memories of home. I would try to plan to have things coming out of the oven just as the family stepped into the house from busy school activities and work schedules. Home-made bread, cherry pie, and on and on the list would go. And they did remember. So I would get my list upon arrival. And of course, being Mom, I tried to squeeze in as much as possible. I do believe the chicken and noodles were always thier favorite.

Smiling at sunrises once more

A Christmas holiday that was a highlight was the year Reagan was born in November. When I walked into Craig's home and saw that baby, it was like Craig had come back in the form of baby. John was only eight, but he was silly about that baby. He would carry him around and feed him. He wanted to make sure all of Reagan's needs were met. Reagan is in kindegarten now. He has his mother's fair skin, but his face is like looking at Craig. He has a sense of humor that just makes me smile. He gets so tickled as he watches cartoons, and it is just delightful.

I always had at least one stop on my flight back to Wyoming, but while on the plane, I would have a book in hand, snoring all the way. Early on in my time with the university, after one of the holidays with the family, something was said that gave me the determination to get on with life. It had been an enjoyable time with the family. I had enjoyed the grandchildren, laughed a lot at Craig's nonesense jokes, went to funny late-night movies with Rachel and Sandy, and just loved being with the family. Sandy later told me what Craig said after I had left: "Now that is how I remember my mom!" Wow! I thought a great deal about that comment. I have often thanked God for my daughter-in-law Sandy. I remember well the college graduation day when both Sandy and Craig received their teaching degrees. She and I have had many delightful conversations about our love for children.

Those times of restoration are vital in one's growth, but there is a point of learning and gleaning, and then getting on with life. Life is a choice. We can choose to be happy or miserable. Unfortunately for those who enjoy their misery, they tend to dump it on to everyone else they come close to.

For many years I taught a class entitled "Creative Parenting." I would explain that when the children leave the nest, they have the right to live their own lives. But the fact of the matter is that we will always be the parent, and we will always love our children even after they are grown. I have come to the conclusion that maybe the best gift we can give our grown children is to just be a good listener, love the grandchildren, show up for the athletic events, give a word of advice (only when it is asked for), celebrate life with the family, share a lot of laughter, and enjoy the simple things in life like chicken and noodles.

God made this human frame of ours. He knew there would be times of sorrow, times when our spirit would need to be restored. Some of the greatest hymns ever written came from a broken-hearted saint, who could hear the melody and words more clearly as they walked their own personal journey with this Shepherd of Heaven. I remember well my dear friend Mary Ellen Fraser playing such a song on her violin, which I had always cherished. The melody, combined with the words penned, have always been a source of comfort. I was grateful to the McClaflin family when this particular hymn was chosen for our father's funeral.

As one pauses to understand the circumstances surrounding the words, it only enhances the depth of passion mingled with sorrow that brought this beloved hymn to the world. Horatio Spafford, a wealthy businessman, lost his fortune due to the Chicago Fire in October of 1871. His family was crossing the Atlantic shortly after this disaster. The ship they were traveling on collided with another ship. Spafford's four daughters were lost at sea. His wife Anna sent him a telegram, with the crushing words, "Saved alone."

Spafford was traveling across the Atlantic weeks later, and as he passed the place where his daughters were drowned, the words of this song came to him. The Heavenly Shepherd speaks to us by his Holy Spirit. I will pen but a few of the lines of this beautiful hymn.

IT IS WELL WITH MY SOUL

But, Lord, 'tis for Thee, for Thy coming we wait,
The sky, not the grave, is our goal;
Oh trump of the angel! Oh voice of the Lord!
Blessed hope, blessed rest of my soul!

Is is well, with my soul, It is well, with my soul,
It is well, it is well, with my soul.

And Lord, haste the day when my faith shall be sight,
The clouds be rolled back as a scroll;
The trump shall resound, and the Lord shall descend,
Even so, it is well with my soul.

Horatio G. Spafford, 1828-1888, Philip P. Bliss, 1838-1876

The human frame does not have a built-in button that can be pushed for patience. When one comes to those pauses in life when time is required to restore that inner person, it is hard to wait. Whether restoration is required because of grief, a major life change, a sinful act, or an injustice, time is required. Everyone has a story. "You just don't know how I have suffered?" How easy it is to fall into the pit of self-pity, which only increases the time for healing. It doesn't take long, as we look around, to find someone else whose trials are far worse than our own. The 23rd Psalm could be a road map for the entire life span, and I am grateful for the brief verse, "He restores my soul," indicating there will be times we need the reassurance of this Shepherd that he can take those broken and bruised places of our lives, and bring us to a heightened level of awareness and growth. Most likely this growth will not come without some pain, whether physical, emotional, or a combination of both.

Those times of reflection when one walks through periods of restoring of spirit are enhanced with the five senses. Later, we can remember a particular place, what season of the year it was. A song or fragrance can bring back a sorrow or memory long buried or forgotten. It is hard to imagine that the Heavenly Shepherd would understand when we are sorrowful and broken hearted. The 53rd chapter of Isaiah has always brought me great solace in the hard times.

Surely He has borne our griefs and carried our
sorrows; Isaiah 53:4

As I pen the words to the page today, my mind goes back to a place I would like to be as I write this chapter. It was a private place where I could sit on a large boulder, fly pole in hand, and hear the late summer sounds of water running down a steep mountain cliff. I often drove up to the Shell Falls when the afternoon heat became too heavy, but this place was more private. There was a pull-out area where I could park my car. It only took me five minutes to drive there from my house. On days I had the luxury of being home, there were always chores to be done. But just to slip away to this private place under the bridge would restore my spirit in such a way that I would be rejuvenated.

*Shell Creek Cattle Bridge on west side
of the Big Horn Mountain range*

The heavy wooden cattle bridge that had been constructed many years ago had been used for bands of sheep and herds of cattle to cross over Shell Creek in order to reach the path that led up into the Big Horn Mountain range used for summer pasture. There was a pull-off area where I could park my car next to the bridge. Cars would whip by just coming down from the switchbacks on the west side of the mountain. Near the underbrush there was a deer trail, where I could make my way down to the water. Even in the late summer, the water was cold and clear. I would nestle in the crevice of the large boulder and get out my fly pole. A friend had been very patient to give me lessons.

I enjoy watching fly fishermen out on the mountain streams. The movement of the orange fishing line making its silhouette of circles out over the water could be described as a symphony in motion. My casting would be decidedly more like circle around, stop, disconnect the hook from the tree branches, and then start the process all over again.

I don't think I ever caught a trout in those little pools at the base of Shell Canyon. I spent more time studying the rock formations and enjoyed listening to the rustle of the leaves in the trees overhead that gave a protection of shade. From where I sat under the bridge, only the tops of the cars were visible as they sped by. It was a quiet sanctuary where I was at peace.

CHAPTER 5:
HE LEADS ME IN THE PATHS OF RIGHTEOUSNESS

Feed the chickens

In those early years on the homestead, every family member had a job. After coming home on the school bus, one of my chores was to feed the chickens. I didn't have a horse yet, so I had to get by with a long stick, with a rope tied at the top to substitute for reins. I made trails out through the weeds and could entertain myself for a good deal of time in my fantasy world of being a cowgirl. One night it was almost dark when my dad asked me if I had fed the chickens. Of course, that was the last thing on my mind. I don't remember so much that he scolded me, but he did sit me down and explain to me that the family was depending on me to do my part on this homestead; those chickens were depending on me. I never cared a great deal for those chickens because they would peck my hand when I gathered the eggs, but that night I began to have empathy for those chickens out in the barn. Later in life, when something would arise when determination and loyalty was needed in a situation, I would hear myself say, "Just get up and go feed the chickens."

WWII

The Great War was over, and not all the veterans came home to their families. I was almost two before I was introduced to my father. He had been a pilot with the United States Air Force. As a child, I always sensed a sadness that wasn't tangible but it was there. While he was flying back to London at night from a mission, one of the wings on the plane caught fire and most of the crew was lost in the bitter cold waters of the English Channel before rescue was possible. A small piece of my father's parachute was caught by the wind, so he was located just before he drowned. As the years quickly pass in my own life, I have wished many times that I would have asked him about his experience. It was a subject never broached with him. I did notice he never swam with the family. I heard him comment once, "I don't want to swim anymore, after my big dip."

When I was doing interviews with the homesteaders for the research project, I came to understand that the veterans spoke very rarely with their families about the war. But they would talk with each other upon occasion. One summer afternoon, I was visiting Lyle and Dorothy French, taping both of them as they told their family history. I had spent a good deal of time with them. The recorder had been turned off, and I was getting ready to walk out the door. Lyle began to talk about my dad. He told me of a time he and my dad were staying together while attending a 4-H conference. It was late at night, and they had returned to their motel room. Daddy sat on the side of the bed, taking off his shoes. He began to tell of the night his plane went down in the English Channel, his voice cracking, as he mourned the loss of all those friends from so long ago. "I didn't want to go back to London that night, felt we should stay, but everyone insisted, so we started out. I was the pilot; I should have listened to my gut feeling."

Lyle came over next to me. "Pat," he said, "I just told him, Wallace, you've got to forgive yourself; it wasn't your fault."

I held on to the door knob of the outside door, looking at Lyle. I was afraid I was going to break down right there and weep for my dad. I managed to keep my composure until I got into the car. I cried all the way home, knowing somehow; instinctively even as a child, there was a sadness about my father that he kept so deep inside of him.

All of the homesteaders in the Heart Mountain community were veterans from WW II. Growing up in that community of war veterans, the children were given a sense of the greatness of this country. Seeing the American flag flying and hearing the national anthem brought a sense of responsibility.

In the presidential election year of 1952, we still did not have electricity out in the Heart Mountain community. One afternoon is still in my memory. Mike and I had come into the house after riding the school bus. Our living room was filled with neighbors listening to a battery-operated radio. The election returns were coming in, and there was great excitement as Eisenhower was going to be the next president. I was only in the second grade, so I couldn't understand all the issues and the whole process of elections and the differences between the Democrats and Republicans. What resonated in my young girl's mind were the awesome privileges we had and the reverence that was given to the president of the United States.

Elections

Elections for the president of this country roll around every four years. Seems in this age of the Internet and all the modern ways of mass communication, it only increases the times of being swamped with political strategies. Down inside most of us, we hope that just maybe this election year will be different, that honesty, integrity, concentrating on the vital issues that affect citizens of this great country will be the center focus. But alas, as the months approach the upcoming election in November and the finish line is in sight, we find the central focus changes into an ugly accusation of character. Which party can be the cleverest in this process of mental assassination of the opposing candidate? The ugliest part of this process is that we find ourselves getting caught up in the fracas. The well-honed speeches can be so full of incorrect information that after a point we find that we are wondering what the truth is. My father used to tell me, "If you can't say something good about someone, it would be better to be quiet." Those words are burrowed deep into my heart, but I can't say that I always live up to the wisdom he imparted so long ago.

In my lifetime, I have followed many election years but I have to say that this year can take the prize for being the most cut-throat. Regardless of party affiliation, there have been nights I have just turned off the news, as I have been ashamed at what was being said.

Because of my son Craig's influence in having an innate understanding of the political scene, our family has a keen interest in the governmental process. On election night, his telephone line is hot. Within our family, we jokingly say, "We need a Craig Fix," when the election returns are coming in. If Craig's line is busy, then my phone starts ringing, and I will hear an impatient voice on the other line, "I can't get a hold of Craig!"

One thing is sure: We love this country of ours. God Bless America! Our family likes to sing and break out in harmony when patriotic songs are being sung, and often the feelings of respect for how this nation has been blessed will move us to tears.

One morning before I began to write, I turned to the Bible passage, I Corinthians 13. I have made it a regular habit to read these verses, and there are times I realize I fall short of the truth in the words laid down as a road map.

"Love is patient, love is kind. It does not envy, it does not boast, it is not proud. It is not rude, it is not self-seeking, it is not easily angered, it keeps no record of wrongs. Love does not delight in evil but rejoices with the truth. It always protects, always trusts, always hopes, always perseveres." I Corinthians 13:4

The 23rd Psalm relates to this Shepherd of Heaven who cares for the individual person, as depicted in the care over a lamb. How much more does He care for all the affairs of man? I have often referred to this passage of scripture when praying for our nation, along with other countries of this world.

"If my people, who are called by my name, will humble themselves and pray and seek my face and turn from their wicked ways, then will I hear from heaven and will forgive their sin and will heal their land. Now my eyes will be open and my ears attentive to the prayers offered in this place. 2 Chronicles 7:14

Coming into this season of my life, some refer to as the "Golden Years," I have come to the conclusion that one of the finest compliments that could be paid as an epitaph, whether it is a man or woman, would be "That person was an individual of principle."

Within the human frame is the desire to find such a genuine person, who truly has a servant's heart.

Eagle's eyesight

Sitting out on the deck, looking out over the mountain range in Shell, an added bonus was when the eagles could be seen out on the horizon. It was incredible to see the majestic wingspan and beauty of these mighty birds at such close range. As they circled around the valley, they could see small animals from a great distance. I watched my small Yorkie with a sharp eye, as the thought of him becoming a meal for one of these powerful birds was more than I could imagine.

I have known persons who were terrified at the thought of flying in a plane; not me. I don't recall ever being anxious before a plane ride. There have been times I have prayed when there was turbulence, or during a long overseas flight when the weariness set in. On flights when the weather was overcast, I always have gotten a certain thrill as the plane escalated up above the cloud mass. Remembering the speed that an eagle could elevate itself with its powerful wings spread up through the cumulous volumes of brilliant white would always invigorate my spirit. Flying high above the clouds, the eagle can look down through the haze to see a minute object. That brings to mind a favorite scripture:

"And God raised us up with Christ and seated us with him in the Heavenly realms in Christ Jesus, in order that in the coming ages he might show the incomparable riches of his grace, expressed in his kindness to us in Christ Jesus." Ephesians 2:6

Just to know that we have been given a choice in this matter is incredible to me. This wonderful life of walking in the righteousness of God, which allows man to have the insight and wisdom of sitting in those Heavenly places with God, has been promised to those who walk with this Great Shepherd.

Alfred Cawston

I think that I am most fortunate when I look back over my life and remember those people who have invested so much in me. I attended

Central Bible College in Springfield, Missouri, in 1964. There was a professor there who is vivid in my mind. Alfred Cawston was only teaching for a year in an appointment as a missionary in residence. He had founded the Southern Asia Bible College in 1951. He and his wife Elizabeth had been missionaries for thirty years. The impact of the work they had done was felt in many parts of the world. At the time I was a student at CBC, I didn't know much about this professor other then he inspired me with a Godly zeal that has always been with me. I took as many classes as I could that year under him.

For several days in the second semester, a time of prayer broke out with the students. The power of God that swept over that campus came with prayer that started early and lasted way into the night. Dr. Cawston was a key figure in leading that time of worship and prayer that was touched with a divine manifestation of God's glory. Upon returning to the classroom schedules, one particular day remains in my thoughts. He was explaining to the class that there are mansions upon mansions of God's blessing that have not even been tapped yet. After the days of blessing the campus had already experienced, I was in awe of this statement.

I never dreamed I would have the privilege of seeing this man again, so I was sad when I told him good-bye at the end of the year. About ten years later, Alfred and Elizabeth Cawston were invited to our home to stay with our family for several days. Our children were very young, and the house was small. I was very anxious about this visit but I was also so excited, as this professor was so dear to my heart. I did not know Elizabeth, but it didn't take any time until all of us grew to love this couple deeply.

Our children loved them like grandparents, as they would take such a personal interest in Craig and Shana. I was pregnant with our third child, Rachel. It had been a difficult pregnancy, and I had required a good deal of bed rest. Before the first evening had come to an end, it seemed as if this couple had become family members.

They spent a great deal of time overseas, but when in the States, even with a hectic schedule, they would squeeze in several days with our family. I would be so excited before they would arrive. The time would fly by so fast, and then they would be gone, and I would go through feelings almost like a withdrawal, as I would miss them so terribly.

They both were such incredible people. The missionary work they had done was astounding, but when they came to our home, they just melted into the scene, taking the children on their laps and loving each of us.

Our family had an appointment one evening when they were arriving. I had put a key under the mat for them, and when walking into the house, Alf had gotten into the refrigerator and was eating some old hotdogs. I was worried for him, as I didn't know how long they had been there, and I was afraid it would make him sick. But it was so much like him to remind me he had lived in India for thirty years, and his immune system was far advanced.

One day when he came into the kitchen, I was down on my knees scrubbing the floor. I was a busy mother of three small children with many other responsibilities, and on that afternoon I was weary. I looked up and said, "Alf, I don't feel like I am doing anything that is important for God."

His wisdom was so practical and yet so profound: "Patty, whatever you do, do it as unto the Lord."

Suddenly housework and the daily tasks of keeping up with a young family took on a whole new perspective for me. I have often thought about what he said to me that afternoon, and it has helped to put life into a healthy balance.

Elizabeth liked to cook, but they traveled so much, she wasn't able to. When she came to our home, she knew we welcomed her cooking. Curry was her specialty. She knew we were not fond of curry, but we would put up a great protest, so finally she would decide to cook up some of her dishes. We would go to the supermarket and find the ingredients she needed. I took delight in watching her in the kitchen, knowing she was having a wonderful day of cooking. The only problem was she would watch each of us at mealtime, wondering why we didn't want several helpings.

Alfred and my husband would take off on their antics, and they would have me and the children laughing into the night. And then when Elizabeth would get tickled about something, it was as if she would explode with uncontrolled laughter. Our family has so many wonderful and cherished memories of them. They are both in Heaven now and missed greatly by their family and countless friends.

Alfred loved his family. He would speak so fondly of his grown children and grandchildren. I asked him once, "Don't you miss your children when you are so far away overseas for so long?"

He didn't have to pause with his reply, "No, because I know they are all happy serving God, and it is only a plane trip away. But when we are together, we have a wonderful time." I have thought of that conversation many times when I see families that live in the same town, and yet times together are miserable.

He would get up before dawn and fix a cozie of tea for Elizabeth. If there were dishes left in the sink, they would be cleaned up. My father was so dear to me, but Alf came close behind.

He had a way of infusing into my inner spirit a love for God. I would listen for him in the kitchen in the morning and quietly slip out of bed. The house would be quiet, as family members had gone to work or were still sleeping. He would sit in the big recliner in the family room and I would sit at his feet as he would minister to me, one on one. The words he would speak would be so full of wisdom and Godliness.

The last time we had one of these quiet times together, we only had a few moments. He looked down at me with those deep-set blue eyes and said, "Patty, when you seek God, pray for his holiness." That is just what I had been asking God for. It was as if Alf could look deep into my soul.

As God looks upon the affairs of man, standing ever ready to infuse into the very fiber of humanity those principles of righteousness, how much better this world would be if we followed his example. From the time of the account in Genesis of Satan and one third of the angels being cast out of Heaven, there has been a struggle for mankind. There is only one God. Satan had the highest station, and yet he wanted to be as God. It is uncomfortable to acknowledge that there is evil in this world, but that does not change the fact. There are those who have given themselves over to evil. We are living in a time when evil is called good, and good is called evil. So many negative voices roar so loudly that one can forget the quiet, everyday people who go about life doing good, loving family, and asking God for the ability to walk in his righteousness.

I have grown into loving the righteousness of God. I long ago learned I fall far short in this walk of holiness. But God looks on the heart, and he sees that desire I have, so life has been a wonderful adventure, as day by day I learn new depths of faithfulness of this Shepherd of Heaven.

One afternoon, after a good deal of time looking over scriptures and making notes, I needed to finish this chapter. It was a struggle to put my hands on the keyboard. How could I possibly convey those deep thoughts of thankfulness I felt? I slipped downstairs to pick up the mail. This Lord, who has been so faithful, has a way of encouraging his servants to complete those tasks he has called them to.

A number of years ago, I found a book describing the last five years of Corrie Ten Boom's life. I loaned it to a friend, and for some reason could never find it again. I have often wished I could find a copy. As I began to write this particular chapter on righteousness, I would think about this faithful servant, who has been in Heaven for some time. I have gotten very proficient at finding resource books, but I had the title wrong on this particular book. One morning, as I woke up, I was thinking again about how I could find this particular reference. I went right in to my computer, hit the search button, and scrolled down through the list of books about Corrie. There it was! The book is entitled <u>The Five Silent Years of Corrie Ten Boom</u>. I ordered the book and was so happy when it came in the mail. I couldn't take time away from writing that day, but as the evening came, I read way into the night.

A few days later, I found myself thinking about the impact God had on this faithful servant, who had suffered so much in the German concentration camps. Realizing my bookshelves had lost <u>The Hiding Place</u>, I again ordered a replacement.

A few days later, the second book arrived. As I quickly opened the envelope, I was anxiously saying, "Oh, I hope its Corrie's book!" As I pulled the book out of the wrapper, there before me was the face of a gentle little woman, who had shown our generations the meaning of forgiveness that only could have come from the mighty hand of God, who sees all the affairs of man.

As I thumbed through the pages, I immediately knew I would have to lay this aside for the time being, as the impact of what she lived through was already bringing tears, and I needed to be finishing this chapter.

Many years ago, before our children were born, we lived in a small community in northeastern Colorado. Our small, white framed church was out on the prairie in a hamlet called Stoneham. There was an elderly gentleman who was a wheat farmer by the name of Charlie Pierce. He and his wife lived very frugally in a small humble home. He was a very quiet man, in his eighties, who would never have bragged about himself. He had a heart for mission work. I found out that this gentle old man would be visited by missionaries from all over the world. He was so generous, but it was never spoken of. On Sunday mornings, I always made sure that I would have the privilege of shaking the hand of this hard-working rancher of the plains. His hands were strong and his handshake let you know you were special. His face had a radiance like he had been touched from Heaven, and his smile was full of kindness, and I would say his life was full of righteousness.

The Good Shepherd knows that we are like sheep that have gone astray, so that is why He is so faithful to come alongside each of us in our journey. The longer we walk with this Lord who loves us so dearly, we take on his nature, and there is a glow that comes into our life, as can be seen by Corrie Ten Boom, and this gentle wheat farmer, Charlie Pierce.

4-H Sheep Tragedy

The old lambing shed full of dust and shadow would seem to give escape from the August blast of heat, but not on this late afternoon. The metal roof, turned to a burnt umber shade from years of Wyoming's brutal January cold and wind, was on this late afternoon a sun-baked oven for me as I worked steadily, combing and carding the Columbia ewe I would take to the county fair.

Summers on the McClaflin farm were filled with long hours of work and 4-H activities. My elder brother Mike, thirteen months older, had a stack of purple ribbons on his bedroom wall from several years of having the great thrill of winning Grand Champion on his prize Hampshire pigs. It wasn't my intent to compete with my brother, but the lonely red ribbon from last year's Columbia ewe just didn't have the same place of royalty in my thirteen-year-old way of thinking.

The suffocating heat pressed down upon me on that afternoon, but the words from my father kept me pressing on, steadily combing, carding, and combing again.

Several weeks prior, my father came in for dinner with that look on his face that clued me in to something exciting that was about to happen. "Well, Pudden, I was out in the pasture and I saw your Columbia ewe and checked her out. I think you have a Grand Champion there." That set the wheels rolling. This was my year. I had worked so hard on my 4-H sheep, and now my time had come. There would be a purple ribbon on my bedroom wall, just on the east side, where the afternoon's sun rays would show her off in all her splendor.

Living on a homestead near the east gate of Yellowstone Park was a draw for friends and relatives from afar. We were blessed with many guests in our home, probably because both Mom and Dad were such gracious hosts, in spite of the heavy work load they carried. Fair time was the busiest week of summer for our family, as we all participated in the 4-H judging activities. My father's Uncle Elmer and his wife, Aunt Lizzie, had come the day before. I had spent some time with them last night after supper, and then back out to the barn I went and worked late into the night. Mike would come out and check on me and help me some, but most of the time I quietly worked away on my Grand Champion, always with my dad's words propelling me on.

My Columbia ewe patiently stood on the fitting stand, her head in a leather harness, as I worked with diligence hour after hour. The late afternoon sun was accompanied by 100 degree temperatures that left me dry and parched. The family was all in the house drinking iced tea and visiting with my elder relatives. I was tired. I was lonely and missing out on all the fun. My thirst reached an unbearable level of Dust Bowl proportion.

I quickly ran to the house, leaving my ewe harnessed to the stand. As I entered the kitchen, I could hear Uncle Elmer telling one of his many stories. I filled a large glass with ice cubes, let the cold water run to the top of the brim, and then stood for a minute by the living room door. One minute turned into five, and then I knew I must run quickly back to my champion sheep.

It has been over fifty years since that late afternoon in August, but even now as I pen the words, I feel that same quickening of breath with what I found in the sheep shed that day.

The silence; where was that beautiful head of white wool? As I came into the wooden framed doorway, the first impact of tragedy was the harness pulled tight around her neck, taking the breath out of her body. She had fought against the tethered leather just enough to lose her footing and had fallen off the fitting stand.

I turned screaming with a cry of anguish. A cry from the very depths of me running as fast as my body could fly, "Daddy, Daddy!" The screen door flew open as my father ran through it, my brother close on his heels.

Of course, they both tried to resuscitate the beautiful prize-winning sheep, but she was gone. There was no way to console that young girl with sun-baked skin for many days to come.

The look on my father's face coming through the screen door has lived on with me, and the recollection is burned upon my memory. The look of concern on his face has come to me at times when I have needed that same mercy and loving kindness from a Heavenly Father, who is touched with compassion too for persons who cry out for a father when they least deserve it.

Sunday morning on snowy roads

One of the family stories that surfaces with my three grown children is a Sunday morning many years ago. It was a cold miserable day, with snow on the ground. What I did not realize when the four of us started out for church that morning, driving down Telegraph Avenue in Detroit, was that in the night, the weather had warmed up, and by early morning the temperature had plummeted. I started up a long ramp, which went over the top of Interstate 96. Underneath the snow was a thick layer of black ice, which covered the bridge. I lost control of the car as it advanced upon other cars in the same condition. Out of my mouth came only one word: "Jesus, Jesus, Jesus!" How many times in my lifetime have I used that one-word prayer with such intensity? Countless times, I am sure.

There were other cars at the top of the ramp, and I hit the back of the car in front of me. We came to a crashing stop; none of us were hurt, but we were all scared. Sometimes I just whisper the name, Jesus, as I go about the day's schedule just because I love him so dearly and it brings me such a sense of tranquility.

I am sure on that brutally cold day out in Shirley Basin, all alone, as my car was about to hit a snowplow, I was sending up another one-word prayer. But as I look back now, I wasn't alone. The Great Shepherd of Heaven was with me, along with a host of angels who had been called alongside.

Scripture tells us that even the demons tremble at the name of Jesus:

"You believe that there is one God. Good! Even the demons believe that and shudder." The King James Version states, *"You believe that there is one God. You do well, Even the demons believe and tremble!" James 2:19*

I don't know that you and I can understand the power in the name of Jesus, but someday we will stand before him, in all of his majesty, and it will be wonderful.

Namesake

A dictionary definition for "namesake" would be "a person with the same name as another, or one that is named after another." This is a compliment to that one whose name has been chosen to be carried on in future generations.

When the twin granddaughters were born, Sandy called long distance, wanting the spelling of my middle name. Elizabeth was named after me, but it is Anna who looks like me. One day I had gone out to Craig's home, and Sandy and I were looking at a black-and-white picture of my wedding. We both were commenting on how much Anna looks like me. Anna was standing by with an amazed look on her face. We have laughed a good deal about her expression. She thought we were talking about the way I look now.

I am grateful for ten fingers, for as I pray in the morning, not wanting to leave any grandchild's name out, I hold up my ten fingers. I am not too concerned, for if there are more children born into this family, I can start in on my toes.

It seems that the term "mother-in-law" takes on hidden agendas, which are not pleasant. I always felt my life had been blessed because of Lenora Booher, my mother-in-law. She not only was a dear and cherished friend, but I knew I could count on her to pray if I asked for her help. Our third child, Rachel Lenora, has been blessed to carry on her grandmother's name. I am sure Mom would be full of joy if she could sit on a Sunday and hear her granddaughter, Rachel Lenora, preach a sermon.

Along with prayers for grandchildren, I pray for my three children and their mates. It seems almost strange to me, as I love Mitch, Paul, and Sandy as my own children.

Shana came and lived with me in Shell for a couple years. She worked in a restaurant in Greybull, where she met a young man who was the chef, and his name was Paul. I knew long before I was told that she was falling in love with this young man. The look on her face was a dead giveaway. She worked the afternoon shift, so by the time she cleaned up, and spent five minutes with Paul, Ha! It would be late when she came home.

I had to be at the office early, so to be able to see the sunrise and say morning prayers; my alarm would be set for me to rise before dawn. Shana's bedroom was downstairs. When she would come in the front door, no matter how quiet she tried to be, she would wake me up. I would say, "Go downstairs, do not come in here," but she would come in and slip into bed and begin her round of stories from the day's adventures. Of course, I would give in to this nonsense, and in no time she would have me succumbing to gales of laughter. The next morning, I would have to drag myself out of bed, but I don't think I would give up any of those late-night talks, as they are special memories now.

Paul and Shana were still living in Seattle when they called to inform me that their third son had been born and his name was Perry Wallace Lewis. He is such a husky, good-looking young man with a charming personality and a flair for music and painting in watercolor. I know my father's heart would be glad, in knowing he had a grandson named after him.

I think every member of our family is musical. All three children took piano lessons, but it was Shana who was in it for the long haul. She continued with the piano, and then she got a guitar and ukulele, and took saxophone lessons. Paul played a bass guitar in a local band, so music has been a big part of their lives. On Sunday mornings, it warms my heart as I see Shana leading the congregation in worship from her piano, and Paul standing to the side, strumming his bass guitar.

One evening I was standing back by the office, keeping an eye on Luke and Maximus while the service was being conducted. The last song of the evening was being sung, and it was lively. The little seventeen-month-old grandchild, Maximus, slipped by me and went over by the entry tile floor and began circling around in the most delightful dance. "Goodness, that little boy has been blessed with the family's love for music," I said to myself. He has such a sense of rhythm, I let him dance.

Before he was born, his father Mitch wanted his second son to come by the name of Maximus. The description in that name says a lot, and the name was well chosen. When he was just a small baby, which didn't last long, he was so happy and had such a charming personality, that he would be passed around on Sunday mornings. Sometimes I had to assert just a bit of force to have a turn. He is going to be a tall man with broad shoulders, so the name fits him well.

I decided early on that this book would be dedicated to grandchildren. As I collected all the complete names, I realized there was a correlation of generations with all of them. Because I have such a deep-seated belief in the importance of many generations of the family, I will list each name as follows:

Erik Steven Booher's middle name is taken from his father, Craig Steven Booher. John William Booher is named for his grandfather, John Arthur Booher, and his mother's father, William Rushing. Anna Marie Booher is named for her grandmother on her mother's side, Rita Marie Rushing. Elizabeth Eileen Booher is named for her grandmother, Patricia Eileen McClaflin Booher, which is me. Reagan Michael Booher is named after his Great Uncle Michael McClaflin.

Kameron Elbert Musashi Lewis is named for his father, Paul Elbert Lewis, and his grandfather, Elbert Lewis. Gabriel Josiah Isao Lewis is named for his father's grandfather, Isao Matsuzaka. Perry Wallace Lewis is named after his great-grandfather and my father, Wallace McClaflin.

Luke Mitchell Ross is named after his father, Mitchell William Ross. Maximus William Ross is named after his father and his grandfather, William Febus.

Enlarge your tent

My heart goes out to parents today, as this is not an easy time to raise children. Of course, I love my own grandchildren, but I also take delight in all the other children in the church. When I walk up and down the aisle of the grocery store, I am drawn to the little faces sitting in the carts. I can't help but smile, and usually the small children smile back. What is sad for me is when I see the look of fear on some parent's face. In such a time, when children are so violated by predators, is it any wonder that parents and guardians have to be so careful? When I compare how differently my childhood was out in the homestead community, where the children were so cared for by not only family, but neighbors as well, I realize how fortunate I am. Throughout this story, I have acknowledged just a few of those persons who have so influenced my own life.

When I think about the mission trip to Africa where the lamby stories were told each day, the faces of children are still before me. In fact,
I have pictures sitting around my desk of that trip as I write day after
day. There were so many hundreds of children each evening as our team
was preparing to leave for the day. I would walk through the throngs of
children, touching their heads and blessing them in the name of Jesus. I
knew many of these children would soon be orphans, and the ache in the
hearts of all the team members is still with them.

Two women who have lived out a Godly destiny for this generation are
Corrie Ten Boom and Mother Theresa. The reason I have chosen these
two particular saints of God is because neither of these women had the
privilege of being married or giving birth to children, and yet they moth-
ered thousands upon thousands of wounded children through the lives
they lived. How many dying orphans did Mother Theresa caress in her
arms as the angels came to gently take them to the Shepherd of Heaven?
We will not know this side of eternity.

I have often read the scriptures in Isaiah 54 about the barren woman
who was admonished to break out in singing. These verses speak of children in desperate situations, yet they want to be acknowledged, loved,
and cherished:

"Enlarge the place of your tent, stretch your tent curtains wide,
do not hold back; lengthen your cords, strengthen your stakes.
For you will spread out to the right and to the left;
Though the mountains be shaken and the hills be removed,
yet my unfailing love for you will not be shaken
nor my covenant of peace be removed
says the Lord, who has compassion on you." Isaiah 54:2, 3, & 10

CHAPTER 6:
VALLEY OF THE SHADOW OF DEATH

Autumn was in its last and final thrust of beauty as the tenacious maple tree in my back yard held on to her leaves. All the other trees in the neighborhood had given in, but not the lemon yellow leaves just outside my upstairs office window.

I delight every year, as I watch and listen just as a quiet whisper, overnight, the leaves fall in one mighty rush of color. The grandchildren come and help me, as we have to get the leaves piled in the street before the deadline pickup and the first snowfall of the winter season sets in.

Recovery from cancer

Virla called one day to say Gordy was taking her in for a physical. She had given the details of what would be done, but I really didn't give it much thought. When she called with the report a week later, the impact of her words did not seem to touch my awareness in reality. What did this mean? The test had to be misdiagnosed. But as more tests were performed, the realization that Virla had colon cancer began to take form. The cancer had advanced to stage three and had passed on to the lymph nodes.

It had been a busy summer going to Kenya, East Africa, with the missionary team. Telling the lamby stories from the 23rd Psalm to the little African children was but a memory now. The picture Virla had painted of Ronnie Jones holding the little white-faced lamb had been the shadow with the inscription of the 23rd Psalm overlaid.

The last leaves had fallen, and winter was upon us. The stories of the lambs would come to me, sometimes in the midnight hours, with an awareness that I had to write again. And now this cancer; it just didn't seem real to me.

I knew I needed to be brave, but I wasn't. The day Virla called and told me she would lose all her hair, the anguished sobs came before I could get off the phone. I was trying desperately to pull myself together but the words seemed to stick down inside my gut, and she and Gordy were so far away in Colorado with their sons' families. My thoughts and emotions were going back to the wintertime of my soul with the remembrance of my father losing his hair as he went through chemotherapy. He had possessed a sense of humor about his baldness, not that he had that much to lose: "Well, Pudden, I hope when my hair comes back it will be curly." His hair didn't come back, and we were standing by his graveside on a hot July day just five months later.

> *"Yea, though I walk through the valley of the shadow of death,*
> *I will fear no evil; for you are with me." Psalm 23:4*

At this point in life's journey I have become keenly aware of how the valley experiences spoken of in Psalm 23:4 bring a depth of insight, if we are willing to look beyond our own personal loss and reach out to another passerby. Cancer has become a common word in our vocabulary, but until it hits home within our family or with that forever friend, we somehow don't grasp the suffocating pain to our chest, as if we have received a swift and deadly blow.

After that summer of 1986 with the passing of my father, I would see women in the grocery store with the kerchief-style hats, faces of gray pallor, knowing they were going through the throes of cancer in some form. But Daddy had been in Heaven for a long time now. I didn't know these women but this was Virla, my forever friend, that creative Spirit that knew the depths of the stories of the 23rd Psalm that had come early that January.

Gordy and Virla had been my forever friends. As I had spent several years working on the homestead research project, Virla had walked with me throughout the entire process. She had been the one who had transcribed the volumes of interviews I had with the homesteaders. Throughout the qualitative research on the homestead community, she had become a friend who knew my heart.

Now here we were, about to walk down a path so many others had walked. I needed to have faith. Not in small measure, but a gift that would come in such a dynamo of power that my prayers would come from the depths of me. Virla had many friends in her church, and all of her family knew how to pray. This was going to take a concerted effort from all of us.

I have had several bouts with pneumonia, so allowing myself to fall into the pit of despair, accompanied with stretches of weeping, was going to have to be avoided. God answered my prayer as the faith came, and along with this gift, He blessed me with the strength to pray in the mornings, late at night, and many times in the midnight hours.

For many years, I have been interested in studying about resiliency in the human soul. What is that inner component that causes one person to survive, sometimes under unbelievable hardship, while others quickly throw in the towel of endurance, lie down, and die without a fight?

I wouldn't say that God speaks to me in dreams on a regular basis, but there have been times throughout my life that He has used this mode of communication with me. I remember the intensity of one such dream relating to my father long ago now, when my son Craig was only two. It was in the middle of the night; the house was silent; I sat up in bed, heart pounding, with my bedclothes soaked with sweat; the heartbroken sobs that came woke my husband with a start. For days, I relived the vision of looking down at the face of my father in a casket. The next week, we went to see my husband's parents. I had always felt my mother-in-law was a special gift, as we were such dear friends. I was relieved to sit with her that afternoon at her kitchen table, drinking cups of coffee. She was well aware of the deep devotion I felt for my father, so as I told her about the dream, we cried together. Lenora was her name and she was a woman of prayer. She spoke with the gentle authority of one who had walked a long journey with this Shepherd of Heaven. "Patty, something is going to happen to your father, and we need to agree together for him."

That visit was in June, and on a regular daily basis, Mom and I prayed for my daddy. It was late August when the call came. My dad was at the state fair in Douglas, Wyoming. He was down by the river watching the judging of sheep, when the heartache came. I don't think he realized what was happening, as he became sick to his stomach, but he walked up to the 4-H office, which was a long climb up several steep hills. He never was one to draw a lot of attention to himself, but he did tell the clerk standing in the 4-H office he needed an ambulance. I will always know in my heart that angels walked up that hill with Wallace McClaflin that day, along with the Shepherd of Heaven holding his hand. His journey on this earth was not over. He had many miles to walk before he was to go home.

He would remain in Douglas for two weeks because his condition was critical. My brother Mike got an early leave from the military and drove up through Kansas to pick me and Craig up, and we drove to Wyoming. Daddy was very weak, but for a few moments when we were alone that day in the hospital, he shared something that is still with me. I looked down at his weather-worn, sun-baked face. In a weary, soft voice he spoke to me, knowing his condition was very touch-and-go at that point. "Pat, there is a man in the next room who has had a heart attack too, but he won't make it. He has given up. I know I will make it." And he did!

It was a long haul for him, as well as my mother and brother, who took over the farming for the next year, but he gradually came back to a place where he could farm again.

I am an avid reader. My writing has only encouraged my shelves to grow along the walls of my study with resources. The Bible always tops all other books for personal daily meditation, but close behind in my files one can find research on human resiliency and many other closely related topics. One book that has caught my attention is entitled <u>Adversity Quotient</u>, written by Paul Stoltz.

I have a great deal of respect for the contribution he has made in research on overcoming adversity. I have recommended this work to many colleagues of mine, dealing with the human resiliency factor.

Long before I delved into the scientific research of those pieces of the pie that make up human survival, I had discovered the importance of creativity in equipping me to endure those hard times of my life.

Through my life, creativity has reached out in many avenues, but my first expression was through sewing. At the age of six, I would find myself buried in the back part of the closet in my parents' bedroom. There was a pasteboard box full of fabric that was my fascination. I would cut hunks of fabric from pieces of multi-colored designs without my mother's knowledge. I always had a family of kittens I would dress up. I wish I would have saved some of those first creations, small dresses with undies to match, with a hole for the kitten's tail. As I went into 4-H at the age of nine, there were grueling afternoons sitting in a hot kitchen in the front of the sewing machine under the eagle eye of my mother. Throughout life, I have thanked her for making me stick to it in those first years, as sewing has blessed my life. When I think back on a childhood of learning on that prairie homestead, I know my brothers and I were blessed. Our home was often filled with 4-H youth. My mother taught the sewing project, and Daddy taught the sheep project.

It didn't take long for me to move into creating my own designs. I later completed a degree in teaching and found myself teaching other children and adults how to sew.

During my tenure with the UW Extension, I had the opportunity of meeting another creative seamstress. Mary Martin was the Extension Educator in Jackson Hole, Wyoming. She had developed a week-long seminar entitled "Quilting in the Tetons." I had never quilted, so I was reluctant to attend that first year, but she wouldn't take no for an answer. It was like a hook in my jaw from the first classes, as I looked forward every year for that week in the majestic Rockies. There were so many instructors I learned from, but four names that come to mind that came alongside and took me on a journey to another level in creativity were Grace France, Candace Kling, Yvonne Porcella, and Elly Sienkiewicz. Fortunately, I came home with beautifully creative books each of these women had produced. Every year, the week would come to a dynamic close with the Fairfield Fashion Show, which would propel me into another dimension of creative design. I always volunteered to go the evening prior to the show and steam press the garments. I don't know if Mary can ever grasp the impact she has made on me in furnishing every year a week so full of coloring outside the lines. Those instructors infused something wonderful into my life that has served me well.

Surgery was scheduled for Virla on October 26 to remove the cancer. Chemotherapy was to begin two weeks later. Gordy would always take Virla for her treatments and sit in the room, holding her hand as the treatments would begin.

Virla and Gordy would try to explain what was going on by long-distance calls but so much of the procedure of all this I didn't understand. What did become apparent very quickly was that Virla was a very sick woman. There were many days I wasn't able to speak with her on the phone. I didn't always want to talk about the cancer but would speak to her about her paintings.

Later Virla would tell me, "I was starving to death." During this time, she shared with me several Bible verses she held on to with tenacity.

"He gives strength to the weary and increases the power of the weak.
Even youths grow tired and weary, and young men stumble and fall;
But those who hope in the Lord will renew their strength.
They will soar on wings like eagles; they will run and not grow weary,
they will walk and not be faint." Isaiah 40:29–31

"So do not fear, for I am with you; do not be dismayed,
for I am your God. I will strengthen you and help you;
I will uphold you with my righteous right hand.
All who rage against you will surely be ashamed and disgraced;
those who oppose you will be as nothing and perish. Though you
search for your enemies, you will not find them. Those who wage
war against you will be as nothing at all. For I am the Lord, your
God, who takes hold of your right hand and says to you Do not fear;
I will help you." Isaiah 41:10–13

"But I will restore you to health and heal your wounds,
declares the Lord, because you are called an outcast,
Zion for whom no one cares." Jeremiah 30:17

Gordy would take her to the Sunday morning church service. They would sit in the balcony and leave during the closing prayer, as her immune system was so challenged during that time. One day a friend, Brett Martinez, caught Virla as she was leaving and slipped her a note. I have copied the note, just as it was written.

"There is a time for every season and for every weakness there is the strength.
We must trust God to help us through that season we do not want.

And walk us into that season we do desire." The Coach

Later, I asked Brett about the note he had written to Virla. He explained that when he felt impressed to pray for friends, many times the words would come that he would put into writing. This note from Brett would become something that Virla would cherish even after she had recovered from her sickness.

One day, Gordy called while she slept. He is one of those strong types of men, not easily given over to tears, but the call that day was heart wrenching. When I hung up the phone, I went into the living room, got down by the couch, and cried out to God from deep down inside of myself. Throughout scripture, one can find that when a person cries out to God in desperation, He runs quickly, just as a parent would respond immediately to the cry of a child in trouble. The Bible from the time of the ancients is the lifeblood of man's existence; but in the midnight hour, where else can we go but to the Lord?

"I call on the Lord in my distress's and he answers me,"
Psalm 120:1

When we look about us and see the wonderful creation God has made and how He truly is our Great Shepherd, why would He leave us at such a time when a loved friend is so close to eternity? Virla couldn't eat, and drinking water was a tremendous struggle. Several times, the medics had to come to the home to give her intravenous feedings because she was so dehydrated. I don't know that anyone can quite understand how prayer works and why God would choose this type of mode of communication with humanity, but He does. I am sure at this point of Virla's cancer journey there was a vigil of men and women who knew how to pray.

Later Virla told me the role Duke, the black Labrador pet, played in encouraging her. He would come up and lick the side of her face, while she spent many hours in the recliner, as it was hard for her to lie down. One evening, Duke was stretched out, sleeping in front of the wood-burning stove in the family room. All of a sudden, Duke sat up, ears perked, his eyes fixed steadily behind Virla in the recliner. She called to him, but he did not respond to her voice. His face was set like a flint, looking at something above her head and behind her chair. "Duke, do you see an angel?" she asked.

It wasn't long into the chemotherapy that Virla's hair began to fall out in large clumps. Her head was cold, so she needed something to cover her, especially in the night. As my prayers went up, I began to formulate, in that creative part of my existence, hats. Not just ordinary hats, but artistic creations. My basement was full of fabric, silk dyes, beads, and on and on the list could go. In all those years of taking those classes in "Quilting in the Tetons" with Mary Martin, I had acquired a stash of wonderful things.

The prayers were so intense that I knew from past experience I needed a creative outlet for my emotions or I would plummet into depression, and there wasn't time for that. I began to bring up my treasure-trove from the basement. There were no dinner parties at my home during this time of sewing and designing, as the kitchen became the lab for dying silk. The dining room was filled with sewing machines, cutting boards, and beads, ribbons, and anything else I could put on the hats. It wasn't easy sewing long distance, as I wanted these hats to not only be artistic, but also comfortable and practical all at the same time. I would come home in the evening after work, eat a quick dinner, and then begin sewing. As I worked with my hands and drew in the colors and textures to form the hats, my spirit took on a calmness and courage as I prayed.

It was a cold January, but the cold that Virla was experiencing was from within, as her body was fighting off the cancer. One evening, as I was sewing, I decided to make a quilt for her. As the textures and designs began to make a pattern, I added silk flowers, and then decided I would use delicate seed beads to enhance the soft petals of fuchsia and purple. Virla is the artist, so this quilt needed to bring a message to a place within her soul that spoke of hope, life, and health. I used a different type of backing, so when the quilt was finished, it was heavier than other quilts I had made in the past. I wondered if it would be too heavy for her, but it was perfect, as she would get so cold, and the extra layer was needed.

Some adjustments had to be made in the chemotherapy. Gradually Virla began to improve. Teddy Jones called and wanted me to attend a "Women of Faith" conference in Billings, Montana, in early April. I had so wanted to see Virla, so I decided to fly through Denver and make a stopover for most of the day. I was amazed when Virla announced to me that she would drive to the airport to see me. I was anxious to see her, but I didn't trust myself. Would she be gray as death, wearing a wig, knowing that all her hair was gone? Would I break down in front of her and cry?

What a wonderful reunion that was. Her skin had a glow about it. It was a stylish wig, and with Virla's acceptance of just a few small tufts of hair, it helped me to mellow out and just be grateful to God in Heaven for His gift of life. We did not spend much time that day talking about her sickness, as we were looking to the future with an anticipation of beautiful pictures she was still to paint.

The chemotherapy was complete just two months after that happy reunion in the Denver airport. We all rejoiced with the Harrells as the report came back of a miraculous recovery from cancer. Life came back to center focus. Virla became stronger each day, and it wasn't long before she was painting again.

As time slipped quickly by, a growing awareness came to me that I was going to have to simplify my life. There just weren't enough hours in the day to keep up the pace of living I expected of myself and finish this story that was so a part of me.

My mode of decision making in the big stuff of life usually comes with processing, and this was one of those times. I knew that I had been given more days on this earth, just as Virla. The stories down in the depths of me had to be penned to the page.

I have always thought a person needed to do things in an ethical manner, so I just breathed deeply, picked up a phone, and called my employer. As I walked into the office of the Broker of the Real Estate Company where I was employed my heart was beating rapidly. Bob Sonsara met me with a smile, but my hands still felt clammy. What would his reaction be to my announcement? At first he tried to encourage me to just take a few weeks and finish the book. I sat there, listening to him, as he made a very good case for the work we do. After some time, Bob sat back in his chair and looked at me. As I began to pour out my heart and describe the passion that comes to one who has come so close to death's door, but must keep going to complete those God-ordained purposes, I was blessed by his reaction: "Patty, you need to go live your passion!"

Wow! How cool is that? It took several weeks to finish up job-related commitments. I asked Bob if I could say a few words to the staff at the last weekly Tuesday morning meeting I would attend. The day arrived when I would be saying some good-byes. As I sat there looking around the room at colleagues, who had not only worked alongside me, but had become close friends, there was sadness. I looked down at the simple poem I had written several years earlier that so described me now in my life's journey. Maybe I shouldn't read it? I have never enjoyed being center stage but the lights were on me. I stood up, briefly explained what I was doing, and spoke about the 23rd Psalm book. In just a few words, I tried to convey how I had been given more days on this earth and went ahead as best I could, reading the words of this simple poem.

MUSINGS OF A DREAMER

Just to catch a glimpse of dawn.
Watch as the lights of day close upon a few rays of sun
As they rest upon the horizon.
See the light of joy on the face of a child.
Hear the laughter of a person loved.
Share the tears of a soul in sorrow.
Have undaunting faith for tomorrow.
Dare to dream in the face of disappointment.
Give a smile to the least deserving.
Hold on to hope when others have let it go.
Love at the risk of losing.
Know you see the world differently and accept it.
Cherish the one who knows your heart.

Patricia, November 3, 1998

The last word of the poem was spoken. The room was silent, and I was at peace. Life has a way of surprising us in the most delightful ways. I didn't expect what would come next, as sitting there that morning, looking back at me, would be some of my most cherished cheerleaders as I came into the most challenging and fulfilling season of my life.

I was back home in my upstairs office writing, allowing my heart and mind to come into that solitary quiet place so that the words would come again. Virla and I spoke often on the phone of the chapters I was writing. She decided to fly to Michigan in early July for a visit.

I kicked into my cleaning mode, feverishly cleaning and organizing. Why do we do this? I don't have a clue, but I found myself exhausted, cleaning out the back end of my closet in the early part of July. I am sure you, the reader, have recognized Virla as a warm and caring human being. With all the things we wanted to share in those six days together, she most likely was not going to march into my house, go directly to the coat closet, and say, "My, my, Patty, don't you think you need to organize these coats better than this?" But alas, in the last few days I had managed to hoe most of the weeds in the garden and flowerbeds, and the garage had been tackled and was immaculate. The basement, being on the bottom of any list I ever wanted to clean, was looking very orderly, and I was to pick her up the next morning at Detroit Metro. I crawled into bed the night before she was to arrive. I was exhausted; my back hurt, my knees ached, but the house was clean, and I was excited.

The day before Virla was to return home, we were sitting out on the deck in the late afternoon. God had been good to us. The maple, so heavy with emerald-colored leaves, formed a canopy of protection from the afternoon heat. This was an old tree, planted many years ago next to this wonderful old home with large windows with oak-trimmed French doors, and comfort. I paused to look up to the height of this old tree, and then my gaze came back to view Virla sitting there, brush in hand, painting. A light afternoon breeze caught her hair. The full head of curly waves with rich brown tones was a reminder once again that we had come up from that valley floor with a story to tell.

For those of us who have come within a breath of meeting death, life is forever changed. Dimensions of time change for us. We realize this life will pass all too quickly, so we must be vigilant in those things we have been called to do.

In my early adult years, through a series of experiences, I came to the realization that I not only loved my own three children, but in fact I loved all children. I will always be thankful for the years I spent as a teacher in the classroom with young people. I have never felt a generation gap when it comes to children. Even though the years have slipped by and I no longer have the physical stamina I once had, just to sit next to a child and teach them a life skill brings me an abundance of joy.

There have been times, as I have pulled up to a red light and seen groups of young people, shoulders drooping, clad in black, with slogans of death slashed across tee shirts, I have been compelled to jump out of the car, run up, give them a bear hug, and tell them they are precious in God's sight. So far I have been able to control this drive within, but maybe someday I will do just that.

Upon occasion I have heard the comment, "There are only two things a person will have to do in this lifetime: pay taxes and die." I have always paid my taxes on time. I don't believe I ever added a deduction I did not have a record of. I have been so overly conscientious on this topic of paying taxes, that last summer, while cleaning my garage, I ridded myself of years of tax records contained in large plastic containers, but not before I conferred with my tax accountant. To my amazement, there are persons who have managed to go for years without paying taxes. I am not interested at all in how they have done this. Going back to the familiar quote, "There really is only one thing that we will all face at some time, and that is we will meet death in one way or another."

Death of a father

One sunny day in July as I sat before my computer I looked over on my desk at a picture now faded with age. As I picked up the small frame, I knew the tears would come, as I could only make out a glimpse of the smile I had loved so dearly from a father who tried, in his quiet way that day so long ago, to give me courage I would need so desperately in just a short time.

I long ago came to peace with the great Shepherd of Heaven with the death of my father. Harboring grief each year on the day he died, July 26, 1986, is not what he would have wanted. But now as I sit quietly with gentle classics playing in the background, I am reminded of that time. It would be easier to pass lightly over this passage in the McClaflin family, but for you, the reader, who is facing that time with a parent, or maybe your own homecoming, I will for a brief reprieve go back and relive that sorrow.

Christmas was almost here, and my parents were coming from Wyoming to spend the holidays and attend my graduation celebrations as I was going to walk down the aisle to receive my diploma for a master's degree. It seemed like a dream, but it was now a reality.

Growing up on that northern Wyoming homestead taught me many life lessons that I still practice today. From an early age, it was understood that my father's greatest desire was to see his children have college degrees. On many occasions as I rose at 4:00 A.M. or studied way into the midnight hours, the look of pride that I knew I would see on my father's face as I reached out to clutch that diploma in my hand gave me a relentless drive.

It had been a blessed Christmas time with the folks, and now they were sitting in the family room as we were about to take them to catch their plane home. My father suddenly had an excruciating pain in his back. He became so uncomfortable that upon arriving home, he went for a checkup. When the test results came back, it was discovered that he had lung cancer, and it had moved on to his liver. He was given two weeks, and the maximum time for him would be five months.

Just as I had done years before, when my father had suffered a severe heart attack, I asked God to give me a gift of faith. Many friends came alongside our family during that time and prayed. I remember times in the night, I would slip into the living room, moonlight creating shadows on the walls, and I would lie across the carpet, weeping for a miraculous healing for this daddy of mine.

One Sunday morning, a lady came up to me after service. She apologized as she handed me a note written on yellow tablet paper, saying, "I am sorry, this is all the paper I had one day as I was at work. This message came to me as I thought about you praying for your father." I thanked her and went off to be alone as I read the words. "Your Daddy has something he wants accomplished and he needs someone to agree with him in prayer." I opened my Bible to the passage she had written down. It read:

"May the God of hope fill you with all joy and peace as you trust in Him, so that you may overflow with hope by the power of the Holy Spirit." Romans 15:13

How I needed to hold on to hope, and I wasn't feeling much joy, so these words became imprinted on my soul.

That night, the prayers changed. I wasn't sure what that message on the scribbled notepad meant, but I prayed fervent prayers that my father's desire would be granted. All the family came to Wyoming in June, and on the last night a long table was stretched out in the living room so that every member to the smallest child could be seated. Daddy wanted to stand and bless the meal and the family. I still had not come to the realization that our father would be with us for just a brief time. It is so good to know this Great Shepherd of humanity, but in the valley of death, He has to be the most precious to those who love him. I am reminded of the scripture,

"Precious in the sight of the Lord is the death of His saints."
Psalm 116:15

A few weeks later, our family was at church camp near London, Ontario. It was already hot and humid that morning during the song service. The minister led the congregation in the old hymn, "I Surrender All." It is hard to describe to one who is not attuned to hearing God's voice how clearly He does speak to us. As I sang the words of that beloved old hymn on that old campground, the reality came to me. That afternoon, I went off alone with an old chair and sat looking out on the lake. For hours, I stared at the water. A few days later, the call came, and my husband booked a flight for me to Wyoming for that afternoon. My heart aches for families, as I now understand the sorrow that accompanies watching the ravages of cancer in those we love so dearly.

Mike and Linda were missionaries in Africa, so it was a concern that they would make it home in time to see Daddy. Later we would reflect on how God had taken care of the smallest details during the time of our father's illness.

One afternoon, I slipped into Daddy's bedroom. He lay so still there, hardly able to speak. The few words I spoke were in such desperation. He looked at me with eyes deep set in his gray face. With a croaking voice barely above a whisper, his words burned into my soul: "I'll never give up hope! I'll never give up hope!" How could I possibly know that in just a short while my faith would be tested as it went through fiery trials, and years later, when I sat out in the middle of nowhere in sub-zero weather with my life on a precipice, those words would flood back as if my father were sitting right next to me in that crushed car. At those times in my life, there was always that underlying remembrance, "I'll never give up hope," and that would cause me to hold on to the Lord's hand with all my might.

The hours before the ambulance came for my dad are a fog at this time, but I remember that Daddy didn't have on the pajamas I had gotten him for Father's Day. I spent hours looking for his gift, and finally decided on a pair: cobalt blue cotton satin with piping around the collar.

Now they were lifting him on to the gurney, his suffering was unbearable, and the faded brown pajamas were frayed around the collar. Of course, I mentioned this to no one. Why would I be so frantic about a pair of pajamas when everything was winding down, and no one could stop it?

In the morning hours, the death rattle came. I slipped out into the hall with the kindly nurse wearing a soft pink sweater, and she explained to me what was happening. All of our family was there that July morning with Daddy. I stood for hours there next to his bedside, trying to put into my memory every crease and line of his face.

When death came, he just dissolved down into the pillow like an ancient gray tent being folded up, then hemorrhaging came, and he was with God.

When families enter into a time of grief, it can take many forms as individuals have their own way of processing loss. Hands down, I have never questioned the unconditional love my brothers, Mike and Wayne, have for me. This was not going to be a season any of us would walk through quickly. Each of us would have to come to an acceptance of this experience. Mike and Linda and their three children walked through their grief on foreign soil back in Africa. Pam and Wayne lived on the farm across the road from the homestead, so theirs was a daily reminder as they would watch Mother.

Mom would drive up to the farm just under the shadow of Heart Mountain, the place that was so close to our father's heart and that would somehow bring comfort to her shattered soul.

I remember having to say good-bye to our mother the morning we flew home. As I put my arms around her, I felt how frail she had become. She was a young widow without her husband of forty-five years.

The Second World War had come to a close. While living in Southern California, my parents had received the news that the McClaflin name had been drawn first to receive a homestead near Powell, Wyoming. They felt this was their special place on earth. They both had worked hard all their lives. I never had heard my father say he wanted a boat. The fall before his sickness he had bought a fishing boat and let Mom pick out a camper. When they had come for Christmas, he had taken us to a boat store so we could see what kind of boat he had purchased. His eyes would sparkle as he talked about his boat and the fun the family would have, all going fishing together. Mom and Dad never got to use the camper.

A few days after the funeral, my family flew home to Detroit. That first Sunday morning after the funeral, sitting through church was an agony. Roy Crossman's face comes to mind. He was a father of six but he often would comment that I was one of his daughters. I remember him coming up after service. He enfolded me in a great bear hug, and we both cried deep sobs of sorrow.

What can one say to that one who is in the throes of grief? We tend to want to have answers, but this side of eternity we may never know why one is taken. As my life has unfolded, I have commented many times while in a place of confusion, "When I get to Heaven, I am going to ask the Lord why." But alas as the years slip by, I am recognizing that when we are in Heaven, standing in the presence of the Great Shepherd, we won't need to have answers.

Prison visit

It was early morning, the family still sleeping when I left. That Saturday morning in early October had a smell of frost, and the air nipped about my face. I would have just as soon gone back and crawled in bed, but then I reflected that I had been awake for hours. It was a sunny day, so I didn't realize the air was full of frost. I slipped quietly back into the house and got a heavy sweater, not wanting to disturb my sleeping family.

I drove to the destination where I would meet Paul Carr, Director of Prison Ministry. We would drive together to the prison. My face was flushed and eyes were swollen. As I looked into the mirror, it seemed as if overnight I had aged many years. Why did I ask to do this? What in the world could I say to those men, in the condition I found myself on this cold brisk morning in the fall of 1986?

Several weeks prior, our family had been invited to dinner in the home of one of the team members of the church outreach to the prisons. During this period of time, I was not a very cordial guest, as just getting dressed and arriving was about all I could muster. We sat across from

Mary Carducci and her husband Tony, listening to them speak of the prison ministry and what it meant to them. I felt ashamed of myself that night, as my own heart ached so badly, I just wanted to go home and pull a cloak of safety around myself. In the next weeks, as I would drive back and forth from teaching, commuting with a van full of children, I would reflect on the words of that very special couple.

It wasn't long before a thought process began to form within me, and I knew somehow I needed to make a visit to a prison. The next Sunday morning, I found Mary and began to try and explain what I was feeling. "I think the Lord is speaking to me about going to speak to prisoners." She was very kind as she replied that she would put me on the speaking schedule for the women's prison.

Now I felt anxious. "I don't understand this, but I feel I need to go to a men's prison." Mary looked at me, with a question mark written all over her face. "Okay, Patty, I will speak to Paul Carr and let him put you on the schedule."

Paul didn't waste any time contacting me. Daily schedules that were packed too full didn't give me time to panic on what I had gotten myself into. The day I would go to the prison came all too quickly. I was not ready or prepared to speak to anyone, let alone men dressed in blue ill-fitting uniforms.

I saw Paul's car in the parking lot off of Interstate 96, where we had planned to meet. As I slipped into the passenger's seat of his car, I smiled, hoping he didn't see that my eyes were swollen from crying.

When we drove into the parking lot and I looked up at the prison, my heart seemed to take a nose dive. Paul went through the process of registering me. It was time to walk through those heavy iron bars. As I heard the heavy slam of metal against metal, the click of the dead bolt, there was no way to retreat. I would have to face those men.

A torrential rain had passed through in the early morning hours. There had been some flooding in the building we were at, so we had to wait in the guest receiving room for an hour. As I sat waiting, I felt cold and then clammy. As the minutes seemed to move in slow motion, I began to feel sick at my stomach. I went into the ladies bathroom and put cold water on my face. I didn't dare let myself cry at this point. "Dear Lord, please help me; the ache I feel this morning is more than I can bear."

I went back out into the waiting room and sat down. In just a few minutes, we were ushered in to a room with folding chairs situated in a circle. About twenty men filed into the room. The service began with singing. I listened to hymns sung by men who knew the Shepherd. They sang with beautiful harmony, which only tended to evoke deeper waves of melancholy within my spirit.

It was time for me to speak. All I could whisper was "Jesus." He came to me with lightning speed. As I stood there looking into the eyes of those men, I did not see prison uniforms, I did not see men incarcerated, I saw humanity the way God looks upon each of us.

I began to speak in a very soft voice: "I don't know why I am here today, but God has spoken to my heart and wanted me to come, so that is why I came. I don't feel up to speaking this morning, so please forgive me. My daddy died two months ago and I miss him so much I can hardly breathe. I know he loved me so dearly and that made me feel so special. The Lord has asked me to come and tell you men that you are special to someone, and He wants me to remind you of that. I know it is hard to be enclosed in these prison walls, but you must remember that just like my precious Daddy, someone feels about you the same way."

From down in the depths of my spirit came the cry. It shook me as the pressure of trying to hold it down had erupted. The men quietly got out of their seats, came around me, and began to pray. As the crying subsided, I listened to the most eloquent and beautiful prayers from my brothers in Christ. The prayers came from men who also had come to the end of themselves. It touched the very core of me.

It was time for us to depart, so I said good-bye in the best way I could. As we drove back to Detroit, I apologized to Paul. "Oh Paul, I am so sorry, I did so badly, I shouldn't have tried to go with you at this time."

Paul looked at me, and the words he spoke gave me a new hope despite the grief I was experiencing. "Don't you realize what has happened this morning? You let those men minister to you, and that has given them a dignity and purpose that is more important than anything that could have been said."

A few weeks later, a packet arrived at the church full of messages from the prisoners, written to me. Of course they were limited in writing materials, but the letters of encouragement and hope they sent gave me faith that the time spent in this passage of grief would come to a conclusion so I could go on and laugh again with the joy of life. One man sent a small calendar with an X placed for each day until he would be able to be released. I knew it must have been a tremendous sacrifice for him to send it to me. The next time Paul went to the prison, I was anxious to go visit the men. It was so good to see them, and because they had shown me such kindness, I was able to greet them with a happy smile, and I think a little laugh came up out of me, as I was filled with joy at seeing them again.

Acceptance

One morning as I strapped on my accordion, preparing to worship in song, an old hymn came to mind. For those of us who have a hobby of gardening, the words resound in meaning. I often quietly sing verses of this song as I make my rounds of early morning watering in the flowerbeds.

IN THE GARDEN

I come to the garden alone,
While the dew is still on the roses,
And the voice I hear,
Falling on my ear,
The Son of God discloses.

And He walks with me, and He talks with me,
And He tells me I am His own;
And the joy we share as we tarry there,
None other has ever known.
He speaks and the sound of his voice
Is so sweet the birds hush their singing,
And the melody that He gave to me,
Within my heart is ringing.

I'd stay in the garden with Him
Tho' the night around me be falling,
But He bids me go;
Thro' the voice of woe His voice to me is calling.
C. Austin Miles, 1912

Years ago, this was a song often sung at funerals. It is common to associate certain songs with life situations. At times, I have heard someone say, "I never want to receive fresh flowers, because the smell reminds me of the death of a loved one." I think of the lovely melodies and fragrances that will cease to be a part of an individual's life, and that is very sad. Life seems to take us right where we are at. If we live long enough, we will at some time have a season of grief in some form or another. Grief is usually identified with the death of a loved one. In fact, grief can accompany many of life's circumstances: losing a home, divorce, loss of a pet, a failed career.

I have had a personal relationship with this Great Shepherd of Heaven, Jesus Christ, from the time I was a small child. That has not insulated me from times of sorrowful grief and loneliness. As I look back over my personal journey, I would not ask for those seasons of grief to be taken away. As I was looking through the computer files yesterday, I came across a poem I had forgotten writing. I am so grateful at this point of my life that I had the presence of mind to date all of my writing, as it has been a context later for me to reflect on how my journey was playing out at specific times in my own passage. I found it interesting that "The High Road" was written just a few weeks after the wreck in Shirley Basin, when I was still homebound. As I examine the words of this poem, I would think that it had been written sitting on a rock at the cattle bridge next to Shell Creek flowing down the mountainside. But in fact, I wasn't able to drive yet, and found myself in solitude for many days in succession. Although I was in a great deal of pain, not certain of what the future held for me, those months at home were some of my most precious times with God. In that season of recovery from the wreck, it was as if I was the one climbing up that steep mountain path in Shell Canyon. The tenacious perseverance and patience I needed at that time had already been infused into the fiber of my human character from past seasons of grief that had passed into an acceptance of life, as it truly does seem to take us right where we are at.

THE HIGH ROAD

There is a path along life's journey so few choose to traverse.
A high road sometimes a great distance
From the well-traveled highways of this life.
A road map of this lane many times hard to read.

While walking this path,
One need take heed as the far distant lane is not visible to the
human eye.

It is the path of faith,
A difficult way of self sacrifice,
An ever increasing personal endurance
That reaches far beyond what can be attained
Within the human frame.
A letting go of those beggarly elements
That engulfs the carefree passerby.

This journey will at times go through craggy cliffs, high mountain
passes;
But when the faithful ascend into the Heavenly trails
It is possible to look down on the valley of human trials overcome.

The air so free from the pollution of this life gives renewed life to
the climber
Who has surrendered himself to difficulties to attain the highest
prize?
All man's senses take on a new keenness,
Bringing with it a clear eye and ear to see and hear God in His
glory.
Patricia, March 2001

For the most part, parents love their children. We hear the horrific stories of child abuse, but most of us would jump over the moon to protect our kids. I try to attend all the school programs for my grandchildren, but that is not always possible. I look around at other grandparents when it's time for their family member to do whatever. We are easy to spot in the crowd, as we swell up with pride. I think we would all agree, we love those little ones more than life. One thing is for sure, we want to go first, hands down. The sorrow that is felt by parents when losing a child is hard to comprehend, but hopefully they at some point can go on with life and find a solace.

From an early age, when children can grasp the meaning of death, they know that at some time in the future they will be facing the loss of their parents. We know this, and yet when it is our mother or father, it is different. How many times have I comforted someone else at the loss of a parent? But when it was my own father, suddenly it took a whole new meaning and depth of understanding.

I have completed writing the portion of this book on going through the valley of the shadow of death. I added two of Elisabeth Kubler-Ross's books to my resource files during these days of writing. Her compassionate handling of the topic of death in "Death the Final Stage of Growth" gives meaning to the seasons that persons walk through in the death of a family member or special friend. I was hoping I could move right on to the next verse, but here I sit late in the afternoon on a perfect August afternoon, with classical music playing, knowing I have to share a time in my own personal journey when I just could not seem to get to the next stage of growth and acceptance. What was wrong with me? I had a deep faith in God. My father was in Heaven. I had many responsibilities. People were counting on me. So for a short reprieve, I will go back to a time in my own journey, and roll back the layers of protection, allowing you, the reader, a glimpse of a time I had drawn the tent of sorrow around myself.

The month before Daddy died, we had brought the family home. The time on the homestead passed too quickly. We were all loaded up in the van but I couldn't leave yet. I got out of the van and went back into the house. Daddy was standing there in the kitchen. He put his arms around me, and I can remember Wayne and Pam put their arms around me too. I should have known that day that the Lord was going to take him home.

If one were to examine me in relation to the fives steps of grief, outlined in the work of Kubler-Ross, I would have fit into the stage of denial at that point in June of 1986. In relation to the Shepherd of Heaven, knowing what would follow the death of Daddy, He was giving me a time of reprieve.

The afternoon after the passing of Wallace McClaflin, the house seemed quiet, although all of the family was present except Daddy. I slipped away unnoticed to the bedroom that had been mine as a child. I stretched out over the bed, unable to cry. It was hard to breathe. I don't know how long I laid there. I didn't hear the door open. Wayne and Pam slipped into the room. He didn't say anything, just stretched out next to me and put his arm around me, and Pam stood next to him. My brother Wayne was a man of wisdom when it came to dealing with his sister. They knew I was going to walk through a dark valley with shadows for a period of time. I call him my little big brother, but I am fourteen years older than Wayne. He is well over six feet, long and lanky, dark hair with a touch of gray on the sides, with a smile that always warms my heart. I think he looks like one of those handsome cowboys in the movies. I missed out on having a sister, but I always felt like my two brothers, Mike and Wayne, made up for it in double portion, along with their wives, Linda and Pam. I think Wayne and I have many similarities. I can just see the look in his eyes, and I know he can read me.

Mike and Linda, along with their three children, had to come to an acceptance of our father's death back in Africa, a long way from the old homestead. After everyone had gone home, Mom, Wayne, and Pam had to learn a new pattern of life as they were the ones that remained in Wyoming. The funeral passed by; we said good-byes to loved ones and friends, and flew home to Michigan. School started in the fall. I was back to teaching, keeping up with a busy family, and going through the mechanics of breathing.

The gift of faith I was blessed with during that season of my father's time with chemotherapy will always be cherished. I have thanked the Lord so many times that He was so gracious to me. A comment was made to me after Daddy passed away: "You're just embarrassed because he wasn't healed after you had prayed so many months." I just let that pass over me, as I would have prayed a thousand times over; I just couldn't seem to get a grip on the ache inside. Another person, uncomfortable at my grief, said after three months, "Are you still grieving? Don't you have any faith?"

The human mind wants answers. If we are not careful, we give answers to questions of this life that might not ever be answered. It is not comfortable to watch someone else walk through the grief process. At these times, we need God's gift of compassion, patience, and empathy. If we try to pull another through a knot hole, jumping through the five steps of grief, that person just might miss a time of solitude when the Father in Heaven wants to share golden nuggets of truth only received in a time of grief.

As the weeks passed by, I would get up before the sun and walk around the block; around and around I would go. I couldn't get that last morning in the hospital out of my mind, the suffering that preceded the death rattle, and then the hemorrhaging of dark blood coming out of Daddy's mouth. Mike had seen it coming as he said, "Oh no, here we go!" Nights were filled with tormenting dreams. Life goes on, so the only thing I could do was go to a quiet place in my soul. One morning as I walked around the block with ice and snow on the sidewalk, I prayed and cried, asking my Heavenly Father to help me cope with the grief. His silent voice came to me that morning. "You cannot think any more about the morning he died; I'll put the memory in a safe room and shut the door." As I stood there on that brittle winter morning, an inner strength came to my being. I walked back to the house, fixed breakfast for the family, and drove the children to school.

I have had to relive that morning in the hospital as I have penned the words to this page, but this is safe time for my spirit, and I long ago came to an acceptance.

A year after Daddy's funeral, Bob and Diana Allessi, formerly from our church in Detroit, invited our family to Florida. We were given the keys to a lovely condo right on the water's edge. I had always loved swimming in the ocean. I would go out in the morning and swim way out into the water. I swam away from the family as the tears would come, and I didn't want them to see me. One evening we were invited to dinner with very dear friends who also were from our congregation in Detroit. They had moved to Florida so it was a special treat to see them. Fred and Georgia King and her mother, Sister Burkholder, who had been my husband's secretary, made the evening special for us. I thought I had managed to be my old self, just like former times, with these wonderful friends who always had been so good to our family.

The next morning, we left early and headed back home. We had only driven for about two hours. I was grateful my husband was driving as we drove through a narrow pass. There was a river on the driver's side and a large rock embankment on the passenger side. As I looked in the side mirror, I saw sparks flying up from the pavement. Suddenly the van began to swerve violently towards the boulders on my side. As John clutched the steering wheel, he was able to bring the van to a stop. When we got out of the van, we were shocked to see that both tires on the passenger side had fallen off. We were later to discover that the lug nuts had not been tightened when four new tires had been put on the van, just before we had left on the trip.

Bob and Diana Allessi drove out to meet us. The girls went with their father and Bob into a town nearby to get the tires repaired. When I look back on that morning, I know God's hand of safety was on our family, as the van could have rolled so easily into the boulders. I am also aware that my loving Shepherd had heard my heart's cry to him that week as I swam out into the ocean. God had given Diana just the words I needed to hear: "Patty, we have all noticed, you are not okay. Your heart is so sad; you are still in deep grief over the loss of your father." Her words were not condemning, but filled with compassion and understanding. The hot tears that ran down my face brought a relief from the weight of trying to lift myself out of the sadness. It was hard to speak, as the cocoon of grief had wrapped itself so tightly around my soul that I had become silent.

But I did begin to talk with Diana, telling her how much I missed my dad.

The next week, the girls were off to youth camp, Craig was away on a job, my husband was at the office, and I was home alone. It was almost to the day, a year since Daddy's death. This grief had to pass on, as it was affecting my life too greatly. I went into the sunroom, closed all the windows, and began to pray. I hope all my neighbors were not home on that day. There have been times throughout my life that I would say I have travailed in prayer for another, but on this day God heard my need.

I could no longer be in the stage of denial because death had come. If it took bargaining, then I would have been willing to do anything. As I prayed, I was shocked as I began to tell God, "I am so angry." I don't ever remember acknowledging that in my life before this time. At first it scared me, as I heard the words pouring out of the depths of my spirit. For an hour, the sobs came in such violent force, and then I was absolutely quiet. I sat there for a long time, grateful for no phone calls, just quiet. After a time, the room was filled with the presence of God. It was as if the sunroom became a hallowed sanctuary. I began to tell the Lord how much I loved him and then asked, "Dear Lord, what has happened to me? I feel like there is a huge hole in my heart."

The Holy Spirit began to speak to that inner part of me reserved only for Him. "The pain you have felt in grieving for your father has been crushing to you. During the process of grief, I have enlarged your heart to love more deeply, to have the compassion that only comes out of suffering." Later I would find those scriptures that would confirm what had happened to me on that day in July.

> *"I will run the course of Your commandments, For You shall*
> *enlarge my heart." Psalm 119.32 NKJV*

I sat there on the couch for a long time, knowing that my Heavenly Shepherd had walked through this time of grief with me. I came to accept my father's death that day, and rejoiced that he was in Heaven with God. As I stood up, I was free. The NIV translation expresses well what I felt:

> *"I run in the path of your commands, for you have set my heart*
> *free." Psalm 119:32*

The weeks quickly passed, and school began again. Some of my happiest moments have been when I was in a classroom with young people. A weight had been lifted off me. I could see the faces and hearts of the students more clearly. But I was different. It seemed as if I had a keener sense of life, not wanting to miss that one sitting in my class, sad and alone.

Shell canyon cattle trail

Years later, when I would drive up through Shell Canyon, I would pull the car off the road, look across the deep ravine, and follow with my eyes that mountain path made by the cattle so many years ago. Linda and KL Reed had lived down the hill and around the corner from me those years in Shell. Linda was a true-blue friend; I often read my freshly penned poems to her. We enjoyed inspecting each other's gardens, sharing the latest novel we had read, crying together when pets died, and just enjoying life together.

I have asked KL about that mountain trail at times, wondering how he had made the trip up the mountainside. "Were you scared, KL?"

"Well no, but then I didn't want to go up the trail very often, and I am accustomed to that type of terrain." KL is one of those cowboys you read about in the old Westerns, as he is a horseman in his own right. I enjoyed the little community of Shell. As I would take walks in the evenings up towards the canyon, I would take note of the cowboys as they would drive by in pick-ups, still working late into the evening. There was always a dog or two standing on a bale of hay in the back. It was a wonder they never flew out, as they would wind up and down those mountain roads, but they seemed to have glue on their feet as they would bark at a passersby.

Shell Canyon is a deep ravine along the mountainside. As travelers make their way up the switchbacks, the top of the mountain comes into view. I call the massive rock formation that covers the top of the mountain Table Rock. It has been named by others "The Tomb," to each his own. When I was a young child making trips up the North Fork with my family, we would identify all the rock formations that had been given names. It took a lot of imagination at times to formulate how someone had named a certain set of boulders. But this is how it is done out West. We have names for boulders, hillsides, and mountain passes.

There was a hill I used to climb just down the road from the Reed ranch. I don't know that it had a name, but it looked very much like a large muffin made from batter that had been stirred too much. The climb to the top was very steep, as I would have to pull myself by the cedar branches along the rocky path. When I finally reached the top, I liked to sit for a time, looking out for miles in quiet and solitude. On a clear day, I could barely make out the formation of Heart Mountain, which is seventy miles away. One summer a drought set in, the rattlesnakes were everywhere, so I decided I better stop climbing up to the top of my lonely hill. If I did get in trouble, I was so far up no one could have heard me call for help.

I have gone back and reflected on the poem I wrote weeks after my encounter in Shirley Basin. I wasn't climbing any mountain cliffs when the words came to me for this writing. I was, however, on a journey up a steep mountain of recovery, not able to see the outcome, but full of joyful expectation, knowing I had a purpose and destiny to fulfill.

There have been times in my own journey in life, the mountain trail of circumstances have been difficult. At times a passerby has asked me, "How do you make it?" The best way I have been able to express my approach to life is, "I get up in the morning, say my prayers, ask the Great Shepherd for my marching orders, put on my boots, and start marching."

As I look back over the journey I have had, I would not want to take away any season. Both in Wyoming and Michigan, when the middle of February arrives, the Southern beaches are looking real good, but the four seasons are so special. I wouldn't want to miss out on seeing those first yellow and purple crocus popping up in the back yard, swimming in Lake Michigan with the grandchildren, watching the explosion of fall colors, and seeing the excitement and hearing the laughter of children at Christmas as snow lays its lovely coating of white on the evergreen tree in the front yard that touches up into the Heavens.

CHAPTER 7:
I WILL FEAR NO EVIL

Fear is a part of the human frame that has to be grappled with. How many writers, painters, or great leaders have given up because fear came into central focus, and all dreams were lost and hope was gone? I remember those first few days after work; schedules were completed and I was once again upstairs in my home office with the anticipation of finishing this book on the Psalms. Fear would come over me, until I wouldn't even put my hands on the keyboard, but I managed to work through those emotions. The first writing that came out of my spirit was penned to the page and with the thoughts that came, a confidence that I would once again have the privilege of expressing my devotion to this Shepherd of Heaven through words that displaced the fear.

What if

My hands are on the keyboard. I have turned my chair, so I can't see the piles on my desk. How many times in the past have I been in this same frame of mind? Knowing something had to be written down before it was lost, to never return. The same fear, how well I know its face, the droning on of, "What If?" What if my mind turns to glue?

What if someone reads this? What if this pounding in my chest isn't real? But then I know what it is, as I have traveled this passageway too many times on my journey.

Just to grasp and hold on tenaciously to that inner strength that has gotten me through many a storm. To acknowledge my faith in a Faithful God who has always been there. Knowing he speaks in whispers so quiet at times, it takes the discipline that comes only through personal integrity of that one who develops character through the crucibles of the hard seasons of life to be able to hear.

Do I have anything worthwhile to say? Is there a painting in my mind, if not completed that will never find its way upon a museum wall to be admired long after I have breathed my last breath? Is there a child somewhere longing for my smile? Is there an elderly lady, hands aching with arthritis, that should long ago be retired, checking out my groceries at the end of a long day? Just a look into her weary face, "Thank you and you have a nice day." The faint smile passes quickly, but she has felt the caring of someone who acknowledged her as a person of worth.

"What if? What if? What if?" I have finally made it to the keyboard today. I knew that this was the morning to hide myself away in my cave of writing.

I have a habit of rising early every morning to say quiet prayers and read the Bible. After my devotional time this morning, I began going through the same agony of blocking out every distraction. I picked up a well-worn book loaned to me by a friend several weeks ago. Many times in the last few days I have read words from this author, realizing I needed a copy of my own to mark up, as every page is full of rich thoughts of courage and living one's destiny. The book had taken on special meaning, as the gentleman who loaned the book had willingly shared with me a portion of his life's journey. I was so moved by his incredible strength of character. He also has books to write. What if he doesn't write down his story? What if he never realizes the impact he will have on humanity?

What if? What if? My attention turns to you. What is that

passion within you? What is that thing only you can do? What if you let life, with all its detours, steer you away from that inner voice ever calling you to a higher place?

If the dream and vision is there then you have been entrusted to bring it to pass. Have a good journey, fellow traveler. I will be standing in the wings cheering you along to your greatest gift that is waiting to unfold.

Patricia Booher, June 23, 2008

I recall a childhood memory of a night when a pack of dogs got into the flock of sheep in the west pasture. I could hear the barking from my bedroom window and I went into my parents' room and woke my dad. He immediately got up and drove over to the pasture. The next morning, my father described what had happened. "They didn't kill the sheep, they just ran alongside of them, and ripped open their intestines." What a terrible thing for a shepherd to witness, in a flock that had been so cared for.

Dogs are in many ways like humans. They can be nice and friendly, but when they get into a pack, with the intent of overpowering a flock of defenseless sheep, all reason is gone. How many times throughout history have we witnessed the brutality of man against man when mob mentality has taken over?

Through the many years that Teddy and Ronnie have raised sheep, they have also had to deal with predators. Ronnie commented on the portion of scripture, "Fear no evil."

"Sheep have no protection of their own except to run away from their enemies. That is why they need a shepherd to protect them and to keep the enemy away from them. As predators attack the flock and scare them, they begin to run. If one sheep gets scared, then the whole bunch will follow, and they may run over a cliff or into a hole and pile up. A shepherd needs to be watchful to keep his sheep from running away and keep the predators and other things that may frighten the sheep away from them."

In previous verses, the importance of walking in God's righteousness shows His caring for His sheep. Man by nature is willful. Walking with this Shepherd of Heaven in obedience is a day-by-day practice. We at times forget that He wishes to bless mankind with goodness and peace.

God is the same yesterday, today, and forever. He is like the solid granite boulder I sat on near Shell Creek several years ago. He is not moved by circumstances. Scripture declares that the very hairs of our head are numbered. The Bible is God's inspired word breathed to us by the Holy Spirit. The importance of putting the knowledge of this book into one's mind and heart on a daily basis has been proven to me throughout my journey with this Shepherd.

> *"Guard my life and rescue me; let me not be put to shame, for I take refuge in you. May integrity and uprightness protect me, because my hope is in you." Psalm 25:20–21*

One of my personal experiences that proved the power in the words of the Bible was when I lived through the wreck in Shirley Basin. The night before I left on that particular trip, I was restless and had a sense of fear. I was standing in the kitchen with my small suitcase, counting out the vitamins I would need for the week. I had turned on the T.V. and "The Hour of Power" with Robert Shuler came on. I was busy getting my travel items ready, when the words of the sermon permeated my thoughts. I stopped and listened to the verse that was being quoted:

> *"For I know the plans I have for you," declares the Lord. "Plans to prosper you and not to harm you, plans to give you hope and a future." Jeremiah 29:11*

Something stirred inside my heart. I went over and stood by the T.V. and began to cry. I knew that God was speaking to me through those words. As I continued packing my bags, I found myself settling down, and began to quote a well-worn verse that had encouraged me at other times:

> *"So do not fear, for I am with you; do not be dismayed, for I am your God. I will strengthen you and help you;*

I will uphold you with my righteous right hand." Isaiah 41:10

I don't understand why some things happen. I learned a long time ago I don't have all the answers. But I do know that God is always with us, and in the hardest of times that is when he becomes the most dear.

From the time I was a small child, I have loved the 23rd Psalm. I am in awe that I have the privilege to write a down-in-the-heart story surrounding this ever-loved scripture. It is not surprising that the day I would be driving into a brutal snowstorm, the words would be on my lips:

"And I will dwell in the house of the Lord forever, and forever, and forever!" Psalm 23:6

"When you pass through the waters, I will be with you; and when you pass through the rivers, they will not sweep over you. When you walk through the fire, you will not be burned; the flames will not set you ablaze." Isaiah 43:2

When I regained consciousness, I was bewildered and so very cold. "What is going to happen to me; am I going to freeze to death?" Then the inspired words from God came to me again: *"You have a future and a hope."* Jeremiah 29:11 As the faces of my family came into my mind, I began to regroup, knowing my destiny had not been completed, and I would survive this day and have a good journey.

I was relieved when the ambulance finally came, as it was getting dark and the temperature was dropping very quickly. I was taken to the hospital in Laramie. Everyone was so kind to me. Steve Aagard, Assistant Director of Extension, and Mark Ferrell, Extension Specialist, who had hunted with my dad for a number of years, went and took all my personal belongings from the car. I never saw my car, but Steve would later tell me, "I don't know how you could have lived through the wreck." I was greatly relieved when Steve told me he was going to drive me up to Powell to my mom's homestead. I don't think either one of us will ever forget that day of driving, as we both knew that many angels had been with me on that cold night in Shirley Basin.

My brother Wayne, Pam, and Mom were waiting for us when we pulled in that night. I had a brace on my knee and I wasn't looking all that good. Wayne was so kind as he said, "Patty, why don't you just go ahead and cry? I think it will help you." There were times I cried from the pain, but I never cried about the wreck, as I felt such awe that I still had breath in me.

A few days after the wreck, I could hardly breathe as the pain in my upper back was so intense. Pam has an insight that has at times helped me a great deal. She took me over to Cody to see the surgeon, and sure enough, ribs were broken. The brace on my knee was so big I couldn't get my clothes on, so we went to Wal-Mart to look for some sweat pants in a huge size. She got me into a wheelchair, and if the long wide aisles were clear, she would race me from one end to the other. It felt so good to be able to laugh with my sister, as I think it was a good therapy in getting my mind off of suffering.

ROBIN RED BREAST

February is winter in Wyoming. The winter sportsman thrives on heavy snows. Shepherds with large flocks of sheep manage to get through the lambing season, and the rest of us hope we can set next to a log fire place in the evenings. And then comes March with a possibility that a few warm and blustery days will let us know winter has almost past.

It was a month after the wreck in Shirley Basin. I was so happy to be in my home in Shell. No complaining came from me, as I was grateful to still be here. I knew it was early for spring, but I couldn't help but look out on the trees, hoping to see the first bud of leaves. The surgeon advised waiting to see how my knees would improve before doing surgery. I was surprised that the bruises had not disappeared. My feet were still a dark purple, and I was for the most part house bound. I was filled with high spirits on this morning as I looked into the long mirror, combing my hair. I had managed to take a shower, what a luxury. Such an ordinary daily process, now took all the energy I could muster. I wasn't discouraged, but the thoughts would come as a question. How would I ever be strong enough to go back to work if this simple task left me so exhausted? Three picture windows filled the northeast wall of the living room with a view of the west range of the Big Horns. At times birds would be blinded by the morning sun rays and would fly into the windows.

As I stood there combing my hair my mind was full of questions. What is going on inside of me? Is there something the doctors haven't discovered? Will my life ever come back to normal? As I stood there, I realized I needed to be done, and lay back down. I heard a loud bang. I went to investigate with Timmy, my Yorkie type dog at my heels. As I went to the front glass sliding door, I gently pulled it open. I called Timmy back into the living room as he saw it and had quickly gone out on the deck. There in front of me lay a little Robin Red Breast. It's wing looked broken and I knew the little bird was stunned and in a great deal of pain. My pain had already reached the breaking off zone, so as I looked at the bird there, his eyes fixed on me I felt a great compassion for him. What could I do? I must put him out of his misery. I had no weapons in the house. I limped back into the living room, went to the kitchen drawer and pulled out a hammer. As I came back on the deck, some how I managed to get down on my knees.

There was no way I was going to be able to hit that little bird. I gently picked up the little bird and cradled him in my hands and began to pray. "Dear Heavenly Father, you know how much pain I am in, please let me help this little Robin." He lay very still as I whispered to him, his eyes studying me intently. I laid him back down as carefully as I could and went back into the house. A few minutes later I came back out, anxious for the Robin. To my joy and amazement he was perched up on the railing. As I quietly came out on the deck, my little Robin Red Breast turned his head back and looked at me. He then lifted both wings and up into the blue sky he flew.

God speaks to each of us in such incredible ways. He will use the smallest things to speak profound truths to our hearts when we need it the most. For the rest of the day, I felt peace and my faith was reassured as I spoke over and over, "Just like my little Robin Red Breast, I will fly again.

"The Lord is my light and my salvation—whom shall I fear?
The Lord is the stronghold of my life—of whom shall I be afraid?
When evil men advance against me to devour my flesh, when my enemies
and my foes attack me, they will stumble and fall.
Though an army besiege me, my heart will not fear; though war
break out against me, even then will I be confident. One thing I
ask of the Lord, this is what I seek:

That I may dwell in the house of the Lord all the days of my life, to gaze upon the beauty of the Lord and to seek him in his temple. For in the day of trouble he will keep me safe in his dwelling; he will hide me in the shelter of his tabernacle and set me high upon a rock. Then my head will be exalted above the enemies who surround me;
At his tabernacle will I sacrifice with shouts of joy?
I will sing and make music to the Lord." Psalm 27

Craig has been a football and wrestling coach for a number of years. Since the season goes into late fall for football, I try and dress very warm for the grandchildren's games. But wrestling is another story, as it is a one-on-one sport. I try and be brave, knowing this is good for the young people, but I think Grandma just turns into putty when it comes to those kids. It was the last tournament of the season and all the schools had come to Napoleon High School. It was a big day for Craig, as he was heading up the event as well as coaching his team. I arrived to a packed gymnasium and was glad I could sit with Sandy. There were four wrestling mats, so it was a packed gym full of parents and grandparents all cheering for their children. John, my thirteen-year-old grandson, had hurt his arm in earlier matches, and now they were going into the final tournament of the season. After his first match, the pain was incredible. He is strong like his father, so he went into the second match and won. By the third match, he was miserable, but won again. If he had decided to sit out the last match, I don't think anyone would have criticized him. But he went to wrestle his final match of the season. Sandy and I couldn't stand it; we went down by the mat. I am sure with all the shouting no one could hear me and hopefully no one noticed. I began to pray that John would be courageous and not give up. I am sure his mom and dad were praying too. He fought valiantly and he won. The Napoleon team won the tournament. John's arm recovered and life came back to normal. But that day as I looked around that gym and saw all those family members cheering for their own children, I couldn't help but think that in future days; those young people would have fiber built into them to face the challenges of life.

Moments in time can be etched on one's mind by those pictures taken by the family member who is faithful in preserving the family story. Last night, it was my turn to teach the children at Tuesday School. I teach with Ben Poxsen, Children's Ministry Director. I enjoy the time with him, as I see the love he has for the young children. They range from ages four to ten. Being a lover of creativity, I always bring some type of hands-on project for the children to make that enhances the Bible story. Regardless of how the craft turns out, it is important to the young children. A memory verse is printed on a label and adhered to whatever we make. Ben comes directly from work, tired, but he is such a great sport. Last night, we used Elmer's Glue to stick fabric to cardboard. It was to be a small replica of the tent Abraham and Sarah lived in, described in Genesis. By the time we got done, it didn't look much like a tent. The glue wasn't very dry on Perry's tent, so a drop or two is probably in the family van.

We had a Vacation Bible School program in the summer. It was all about pirates. Many people in the congregation helped to decorate for the occasion. It was a huge success, as the children are still talking about it. They learned many wonderful songs. Ben brought the CD up to the children's church room. Every Tuesday night the children want to listen to the CD, sing along, and do all the actions.

Last night was my night to fix a meal for the youth group. When it is my turn, I fix chicken and noodles, as that seems to be a favorite. I spent most of the day writing, telling myself I have the process of making the soup down to a science. I can whip out a large roaster of chicken and noodles in a short amount of time, but on the way to church, fatigue began to set in. I breathed deeply and headed upstairs for the children's class. I was organizing the tent project, as the children sang along with their pirate CD. I went over and sat down and watched the children. Four of those youngsters just happen to be my grandchildren, but all of the children call me Grandma. Mitch and Rachel's four-year-old son Luke was holding a microphone, singing, "My God is so big, so strong and so mighty, there's nothing my God cannot do." The other children were on the area rug singing along and flexing their miniature muscles. As I listened to Luke, such a serious face, singing all the words with perfect pitch, I said, "Ben, we have got to get a video of these children singing." It was one of those moments in time. Knowing the powerful words concerning God's strength were being placed deep in the hearts and minds of those young children refreshed both Ben and me.

There have been times I have sat with a client, or parent, and at times friends who have lost a child to teen suicide. What can one say when the parent tries to communicate the depth of sorrow they feel? There will be no more sports tournaments for their child, no grandchildren to look forward to, and no dreams that will become reality for that child. In those times, I have spoken very few words, but have become a listener and prayed the parents would somehow be able to take deep breaths at some time in the future.

I feel I have been given a gift as I look over the shelves in my own library of books on resiliency. I have listed some of my favorite resources that I have been able to apply in the work I have done with families. Why someone comes to the place that life becomes so hopeless is an interesting question.

When fear has come into my life, accompanied with a sense of hopelessness, I have run quickly to the Shepherd of Heaven. But of course, I knew I had the opportunity to do this. I am sure the passion that burns within me to complete this manuscript is heightened with the desire to share simple stories of life that might just give someone else a sense of hope, when despair has overtaken them.

Puppy dogs and other canine friends

At times, I have pondered the kindness of God in having the idea of pets. My particular brand of creature from the animal kingdom comes in the form of a very small Yorkie-type dog named Timmy. His mother Katie had two litters of puppies. Timmy was the smallest pup in the first batch of four. A gentle nature accompanied his small frame, so of course he had to stay with me. A year later almost to the day, Katie had another litter of four puppies. I built a ridiculous-looking fort by the front door of the house for the little creatures while I was away at work during the day.

Katie was an incredible mother. I was amazed at her dedication to these little puppies. But the second time around, she didn't have the energy she possessed the year before. I had put a porta-carrier inside the fort for her and her puppies to sleep in. Timmy became the great watchdog. He would sit on top of the carrier and watch all the antics of the small puppies. At times, he would jump down and bring order to the little pack. The second litter of puppies was born late in October. I had decided to make my two oldest grandsons quilts for Christmas. I had multi-colored two-inch strips of cotton lined up on the floor by the sewing machine, ready to sew in the evenings. Since the puppy fort was built by the front door, I would have to walk around the deck and enter the house by the sliding glass doors in the evening.

I felt like a mother that has to go back to work and leave her newborn with another caregiver. What was I missing out on? What new skill were those little puppies learning while I was away in the office during the day? After work, I would go directly home, but it would be dark as I drove into my driveway. I would quickly walk around the deck and turn on the living room light, expecting to see sleeping puppies cuddled up next to their mother, Katie.

One evening is etched in my memory. As I entered the sliding door, I reached over on the wall and flicked on the light and gasped. The puppies were in the porta-carrier, snuggled up to their mother, innocently sleeping, but the carnage through the house took the rest of the evening to clean up. The rich foliage of the rubber plant placed strategically by the window to catch the morning sun's rays was now lying all around the living room. A kaleidoscope of rich blues, greens, reds, and lemon yellow strips of cotton ran from underneath the table and criss-crossed the entire room. I walked over to my well-planned fort. Everything was intact. How did they get out?

I had stayed up too late the night before, playing with puppies and sewing, plus the day had been hectic at the office. There was nothing else to do but begin rolling up the cotton strips and try as best I could to salvage the little mutilated plant. Every once in a while, I would go over and look at my fort. I got down on my knees, going over every inch, trying to find the escape route. Even as small as they were, they somehow knew not to reveal their secret while I was present. The next morning, I was careful to have everything off the floor. The next evening, no rainbow of colored strips, but there was evidence that the little plant had been bombarded again. The second evening was spent crawling around the fort, feeling with my hands, looking, watching those little puppies.

The third day, while at work, I came up with a plan. It was Friday, so I could spend more time in this great investigation of the criminal puppies. As I entered the house that evening, the puppies were safely in their fort; I began to wonder if they could hear me drive up. I warmed up a bowl of chili, laid out the blanket, and put all the round bellies next to me and played for quite a spell. Then I put them safely away in the fort, went over and turned out the light, and very quietly sat down in my rocker by the window. I sat very still in the night hours. It wasn't long before I heard the patter of little feet running. I reached over and flicked on the light just as the last little tubby was running through the baby guard. I went over, and sure enough those little puppies with razor-sharp teeth had cut small openings that would lie flat, but would allow them to slip through unnoticed to their playground of plants and color.

All the puppies were given to loving families except Timmy. He was the smallest of both the litters, only weighing about four pounds. He just seemed to have that gentle little spirit that had to stay with me. He is such an adorable dog; he has pointy ears with the Yorkie-type hair that sticks up; and he basically runs the house. I don't think my children are that enamored with him, but the grandchildren think he is a fine dog.

I have found a dog trimmer that I go to exclusively now, as two summers ago, upon returning to the dog hairdresser, I cried out in dismay when Timmy was brought to me. All of his hair had been shaved, including the long hair on his ears. He looked like a scrawny little rat. It was awful for both of us, as he knew his finest attribute of cuteness had been taken from him. For months, the morning routine would be to check those ears, as the hair very slowly began to grow again.

Katie was with me during those first beginnings of my writing. Pets have an instinctive awareness of their master. Those weeks after back surgery were a trial to be sure. The pain was hard to manage, but I tried to get by with a minimum amount of pain medicine. As I began to write those first poems, the concentration needed helped me to focus on something other than the pain day after day. Katie sat on the recliner with me, always careful not to press next to me.

A few years later, when recovering from the car wreck, Katie had been killed. I grieved terribly at her loss and I was concerned for Timmy, but we both managed to become adjusted after a time. By now I was well on my way in writing the homestead book. I began writing some short stories in those early months. But the thing that I most remember during that time was the prayers that were coming out of the depths of me. While I would make my rounds praying in adoration and thankfulness that I was still alive, Timmy watched. I had some worship CDs I would listen to as I prayed. Timmy has an ear for music, for as the songs began to play, he would jump on the back of the couch. He didn't bark; he just waited. As I would get caught up in praying, I would forget about him. As I would pass by the back side of the couch, he would put out his little furry paw. Of course, I would pick him up and cradle him down inside my arm.

At times, I would go in and get down by the side of my bed. Timmy would quietly come in, jump on the bed, and sit next to me. If tears came in those times of prayer, he would reach his face close to mine and lick the tears away. I have made the comment at times, "Timmy is more in tune with the Holy Spirit than some people." Many times when the writing becomes intense, Timmy will come along side and want to sit on my lap. I have often thanked the Lord that he had the idea for pets, as they bring such a wonderful component into the home.

Rusty Rescues Wayne

I've always felt one of the special parts of growing up on a farm was the privilege of having a variety of pets. Mom tended to lean toward the kittens. Daddy had a sheep dog named Rusty. Like the other farmer's dogs in our community, Rusty had a special place in the front seat next to my dad. In those years, aluminum tubes were used for irrigation. I used to help pick up the tubes and carry them to the next field, but Mike was the one who could get the suction of water from the ditch up into the tube and down the irrigation rows. I never did get a good handle on that job.

Rusty was Daddy's shadow. He would run up and down, chasing the water as it was turned into the ditch. Watching this dog in his play always brought a great deal of enjoyment to our father. Rusty would be covered with mud when the old pick-up returned to the house. In those days, the living room had hardwood floors. It was a big job keeping up the waxed shine with dogs and many other things coming into the farm house. Over by Daddy's rocking chair was a spot easily detected where Rusty, his faithful sheep dog sat.

He not only was a trusted pet, but Rusty was a working sheep dog. He would be called a herder-type dog. He could run out and gather up a flock of sheep in no time. At times, I would take him to the field with me as I watched out for the sheep. It was a great help, until my dad would come out of the house. We could be in the back pasture, but if Rusty saw him, I was sunk, as off he would go, running to the house to be with Daddy.

One day, a rainstorm had passed over. I was out in the field with a flock of ewes. Rusty was gathering them up for me. An old ewe decided she was going to head for the fence. On the other side was a new crop of alfalfa that was wet from the storm. I had previously known what would happen if the sheep got into the field. This was a stubborn old ewe. I tried to get ahead of her, but she was obstinate, and she managed to get through the fence. Unfortunately, many other sheep began to follow her. I sent Rusty running as I tried to get the sheep turned around. At the same time, my dad came out of the house. Off Rusty ran, as fast as he could. I called and called, so disgusted with the situation. Daddy brought him back out to the field, but by then the sheep had gotten through the fence and were eating the wet alfalfa by huge mouthfuls. Before it was over, sheep were falling all around, bloating, and before we could get to them, they were dying. I was a very disappointed shepherd girl on that day, as I watched how the sheep suffered as they died. Death comes quickly, so the old stubborn ewe, along with all of her followers, paid a heavy price.

When the irrigation project was designed out on Heart Mountain homestead community, canals were used to transport water for irrigation from Buffalo Bill Dam, west of Cody, Wyoming. There were canals next to each homestead unit, as well as a large, fast-moving canal called Alkali Drain, which ran through the back of the McClaflin farm. It was a runoff of wastewater from the farms along the canals. A good deal of water ran down this canal, and there were some deep holes. Parents were always concerned for the safety of their children because of the canals.

One day in early spring, when Wayne was barely three, he was playing out in the front yard. Mom kept an eye on him as he played, but then when she looked out he wasn't there. She went out right away, feeling something was wrong. She looked everywhere, calling him. She looked in all the barns, calling and calling, "Wayne!" She began praying, feeling frantic, and worrying about the canal out in front of the house. The hired man, Dale Watts, came to the house and began to help Mom search. As he went out by the sheep shed, he heard Rusty barking way off in the distance. He went out in the back of the shed and could see Rusty way down by Alkali Creek. He began to run as fast as he could, as the dog was barking furiously. Rusty was running back and forth, jumping in the air, way down by Alkali Creek.

When Dale got down to Rusty, the dog was jumping on him, barking and barking, and then began to run off down the canal road. Dale ran, now feeling panic. When Dale came to where Rusty was running, he could hear Wayne crying. He looked down at the canal and saw my little brother down in the cold water, trying to pry his little coat loose. He was so scared and cold from the rushing water. As he had struggled, he had dug himself deeper and deeper until he was in a very desperate situation. Dale tore his coat loose from the fence, picked up Wayne, and hugged him tight as he was carried back to the house. And of course, good old faithful Rusty was following right beside him, watching out for that little boy, who is much taller than me today.

The Happy Dog Jango

A memory I will look back on fondly was watching Paul and Shana as they found the home they wanted to buy. On impulse, I drove by a home late in the day, and thought Shana might want to see it. She was crying before she got out of her car. We called Paul on the cell phone, and it was obvious there was a broad smile on his face as he drove up the street. It was the perfect home for their family. They stayed with me for a few days before closing, so it gave me an indication of what Paul would be doing in a short time. Every night, he would have me up in the office, showing me different types of dogs on the Internet. They decided it would be wise to wait a few months but I knew it wouldn't happen. A common denominator between Paul and me is that we love dogs. There is no rational reason for this interest in dogs, but if you fall into this category, you know what it is like. A few days after they had settled in, I got the call. I drove over to see a little Australian Shepherd that looked like a small sheepdog, with a white stripe down his face, who had been named Jango. A very lovely dog, I might add, and very rambunctious. Paul thought his little dog would quietly set by his chair at night, but that was not going to happen, as he was all over the room, playing with the boys.

Shana prays a great deal, asking God to give her that very special love for the little dog. I don't know if her prayers have been answered to the degree that Paul would hope. When Paul and I do have a few minutes, we tell stories to each other about our dogs with great enjoyment.

Teddy and Ronnie have always had dogs on their sheep farm. These dogs are not like Timmy, who basically is just a ball of fluff. All the dogs on the Jones farm are working dogs. They have had several Great Pyrenees guard dogs that watch over the flocks of sheep and chase off predators. The latest guard dog is Dolly, who is still young. She is such a character, and I have a hunch that down the road I will be writing some stories about her. Nick and Breeze are Border Collies, and they are herding dogs. It is so interesting to watch them with Ronnie as he gathers his flocks of sheep.

I had Ronnie explain to me the importance of the working dogs on a sheep farm.

"Shepherds use a herding dog. And a shepherd can handle 1,000 sheep with one dog or two and bring the wayward sheep back into the flock or at least attempt to bring them back. If the sheep move away from the flock, then they of course are subject to predators killing them. The shepherd protects the flock by moving them into an area where they can't be bothered by predators. As we think about Jesus as our Shepherd, we also need to think of the workers who Jesus called in Matthew to help with the harvest. We need to think of them as the helpers to keep that flock moved away from the evil one. And as I think about the herding dogs, that is their job. I think that we need to also include that in our job description."

"Then we think about the guarding dogs who are out there when the shepherd may not be right next to the flock, and those guarding dogs which are large dogs who are pretty much self-trained and just guard the sheep against the predators. They are there to scare off and keep the predators away, as the shepherd isn't there to guard the sheep himself. So that's why we have the guarding dogs and herding dogs."

Elk Hunting trip

Some of the homesteaders in the Heart Mountain community came from local areas, but most of the families came long distance to claim a unit. That first year away from family was hard on everyone. We all felt homesick, so within our community was created a sense of family. The McClaflin name was the first application that was drawn for the homestead project. I remember our mother often said, "Wallace and I just felt that God had blessed us, and this was our chance to have a farm." When they came to Powell for the interview process, they were accepted as candidates to choose a farm.

Families in the community opened up their homes for these young veteran families. My parents stayed with a delightful lady named Mrs. Bosley. They were introduced to her daughter Bessie Hoff, and her husband Felix and daughter Phyllis. That was the beginning of a lifelong friendship. They became our long-distance family. They had a ranch up near the foothills of the Beartooth Mountain range. Christmas was spent with the Hoffs in the old log home in the Paint Creek Valley.

Phyllis was six years older than me, and I thought she was the most beautiful and important person in the world. She felt like Mike and I were her little brother and sister. When I was in the fourth grade, Melanie Hoff was born and then two years later Colleen Hoff was born, and so they were like my little sisters.

Clearing off sagebrush and beginning a farm out on the prairies of northern Wyoming meant long, exhausting days. The few times we did get to go to Paint Creek in the summer were special times for our family. Felix would saddle up the horses and Phyllis, Mike, and I would ride off for great imaginary adventures up in the rocky ledges.

Late in the fall, Dad and Mom would go hunting with Felix up on Bald Ridge. There was a deep ravine called the natural corral. There were several deer paths down into this deep ravine, but if it began to snow, one did not want to be caught in this area as the massive rocky cliffs made an enclosure that was impossible to get out of.

When interviewing Mom, this is one of the stories I wanted her to share.

"The most memorable hunting trip for Wallace and I was with Felix Hoff. We went up to an area near Pat O'Hara creek and set up camp with tents, and brought horses with us. That first night of camping, the men had put the tents right on the edge of an old abandoned sawmill. The wind came up in the night, and the sawdust blew right into our faces. The next morning we got up early and rode the horses up on the top of Pat O'Hara. I remember how cold it was and I wasn't about to complain, as I was so glad to get to go on this hunt with the men. My face got wind-burned that first morning out."

"The temperature began to drop during the day, and Felix became concerned about his house on Paint Creek, as he was afraid the pipes would freeze. It was the last of October, and it seems that back in those years it got colder a lot faster in the fall. We rode over Bald Ridge and down through the natural corral to get to his ranch. We spent the night, and the next morning we were going to ride back up to the camp. During the night, it began to snow. The men asked me, 'Do you want to stay here at the ranch?' I wasn't about to stay there and miss out on the hunt. 'No, I'm not staying here, I'm going with you.'

"We began the trip back up to our campsite. We took the horses up through the natural corral. There were only two ways to get in. There was a trail below the corral, and up on top, a horse could come down a narrow passageway. It was a rock formation that encircled about a hundred acres deep within the ravine. It was a good place to hunt for deer and elk. Fortunately for Wallace and me, Felix had hunted this territory for years, and knew all the trails.

"We decided on our way up to the camp we would hunt down in the natural corral. Wallace and I took the horses, and Felix went on ahead to spook the elk down into the ravine. Felix left us about 11:00 A.M., and after a long while, Wallace began to get nervous, as the snow was coming down so heavy. A heavy fog was rolling into the canyon, and we had no way of knowing how to get out. We kept trying different paths, but would come right up against the rock ledges. The snow was up to the bellies of the horses, so Wallace thought he would leave me with the horses, and try to get out on foot. But he came back in just a few minutes. 'Edna, it is getting so cold and I don't know if I could ever find you; we had better stay together.'

"About 4:00 P.M., we heard a gunshot. It sounded like it was right above us. We answered with a shot back. Felix shot back and then he started calling us. He was up on top of the ledge, so he guided us up out of the corral. When we finally joined Felix, he told us the only way we would get off the mountain was to follow the fence line.

"Felix was a good guide. He found the fence and we followed it. We came up on a big herd of elk, but we knew our situation was serious. There was no way we were going to try and shoot one. At about 9:00 P.M., we got into camp. Felix said, 'If we don't try and get out, we will be stuck up here for the winter because all the roads will be closed.' We didn't have a four-wheel drive, just the old Dodge pick-up loaded with rocks for weight. We were all just starved so we quickly ate something and loaded everything in the back of the pick-up. Felix instructed us to turn the horses loose, as he said they could find their way back to the ranch. Sure enough, a few days later, they returned home.

"The camp was about a mile from the road. Felix got on one side and I got on the other, and Wallace drove. We shoveled a path for the wheels because the snow was so deep. It was the old dirt road, not the one that we drive today going to Sunlight. We needed to go to the top of Dead Indian, which was about five miles away."

"Felix and I would sit on the back end and Wallace would drive a little ways and the chains would break. There was some baling wire in the back we used to tie the chains together. They kept breaking, and we would just be inching along. We got into Paint Creek ranch about 2:00 in the morning. I can still remember how relieved we felt when we drove down the hill and saw the old ranch house. Wallace and I never forgot that trip. I think we both gained an awareness of the mountain storms and how they needed to be respected. Without a good guide, we would have been lost and probably would have frozen to death up there in the canyon. We had many good hunts with Felix in the years to come, but never had another experience that was as frightening as our first hunt in the natural corral."

Felix and my parents spoke of that special elk hunt many times through the years. As I think about the circumstances of that trip down through the natural corral in such a heavy snowstorm, I can't help but feel there was a Heavenly presence guiding Felix and my parents to safety.

Your rod and staff, they comfort me

Ronnie brought out his staff and showed it to me and then began to explain how it aids him with his flocks of sheep.

"When we think about the rod and staff, the rod is used to protect the sheep from damage from predators or other bad things that might happen to the sheep. And the staff, of course, is used to help protect the sheep and also to catch them to be able to doctor whatever illness they may have, whether it would be lameness or some kind of cuts or damage around the head and to also possibly protect them from flies and other pesky things that might bother them."

"The staff is usually a stick with a curve on one end that can also be used to catch the sheep and bring them back into the flock when they might attempt to stray. They can be caught fairly easily, usually around the neck. It doesn't hurt but the sheep can be turned and brought back into the flock."

After Ronnie and I were finished taping his interview, he took me out to the corral with his sheep dog and his staff. Later, when I reviewed the video taken of his demonstration of how the staff is used, it made me aware of its importance in protecting the sheep. He would go near the flock and, with his staff, pull out one sheep. This is used when a sheep needs to be taken care of. If flies are troubling the sheep, ointment can be applied to the head. The staff does not hurt the sheep, but it is a good way to work with sheep individually.

While living in Shell, I would see the sheepherders out on the mountainside, leaning on their staff, watching over their flocks of sheep. The staff is usually made out of wood. Sometimes, they are carved into ornate designs. In Bible times, the staff was a very important tool herdsmen used with flocks of sheep.

The rod is carried by the herdsman to protect the flock from predators. I once had the privilege, while in Kenya, East Africa, of watching some Maasai herdsmen demonstrating their ability to throw the rod, which can bring a deadly blow to a predator. In modern times, the rod would be referred to as the gun carried by ranchers when working out on the range with cattle and sheep.

While living in Shell, it was not unusual to see coyotes coming in close to the sheep in the pastures, and they certainly were close by in the high mountain ranges. If one coyote is visible, there are usually several others close by. They will circle around a defenseless sheep that has wandered off, and without the close watch of a shepherd, a good number of sheep can be killed.

In all the years I traveled through the mountain ranges of Wyoming, I have only seen one wolf, and it was in Yellowstone Park. I would not want to be out walking and come upon a wolf, as they are very dangerous. One morning, I found footprints of a mountain lion outside the house. I had been coming home every evening after work and taking long walks up into the hills. A rancher told me the lion wouldn't bother me, but after that

I quit walking. When I walked down to the post office to get my mail, I would take a long tree branch, which could be considered a rod, and stay in the middle of the road because as I walked down the hill, rattlesnakes would sometimes be crossing the pavement. I enjoyed living near the mountains in Shell, but I always knew I needed to be wise and pay attention to my surroundings.

It is noted, in this verse concerning the rod and staff, not only does the Lord want to protect us, but bring us comfort as well. The staff can be a demonstration of the inner man, where the word of God is our light and guide in the path to righteousness. The rod can serve as that protection from outside forces that draw us away from the voice of the Holy Spirit that watches over us continually. The Lord warned of those who would come to deceive His lambs:

> *"Watch out for false prophets. They come to you in sheep's clothing, but inwardly they are ferocious wolves." Matthew 7:15*

The teachings of Christ in the three years He walked on this earth ministering are still with us, written under the inspired hand of the prophets. He knew what was ahead for His twelve disciples, and He gave a warning:

> *"I know that after I leave, savage wolves will come in among you and will not spare the flock." Acts 20:29*

A great deal has been invested in you and me, and God is not willing that any man is destroyed. One of the most useful tools given to mankind is prayer. The Lord can touch hearts that are hardened and cause them to be as soft clay in the potter's hand.

> *"Humble yourselves, therefore, under God's mighty hand, that he may lift you up in due time. Cast all your anxiety on him because he cares for you." 1 Peter 5:6 & 7*

It is the desire of the Heavenly Shepherd to bring peace and comfort, and the way this is possible is to have a tender heart in the presence of God.

"Create in me a pure heart, O God, and renew a steadfast spirit within me. Do not cast me from your presence or take your Holy Spirit from me. Restore to me the joy of your salvation and grant me a willing spirit, to sustain me." Psalm 51:10–12

We hear the comment, "There is nothing new under the sun," and for the most part that is true. Satan has not changed his tactics from the dawning of time. Therefore, we do not have to be afraid, but just as I was careful of predators while living in Shell, we need to honor this God who sent His son, that we might have life and have it more abundantly.

"Be self-controlled and alert. Your enemy the devil prowls around like a roaring lion looking for someone to devour. Resist him, standing firm in the faith, because you know that your brothers throughout the world are undergoing the same kind of sufferings."
1 Peter 5:8

CHAPTER 8:
You Prepare A Table For Me

Many years ago, when our young family had moved into a new area, we experienced an evening that was very frightening. We were hungry for grilled hamburgers, so we bought a small hibachi and briquets. There was a lovely park with a creek meandering through it, just a few miles from our home. We loaded up the children and had the picnic supplies in the trunk. We were all hungry, and it seemed like it took forever for the coals to get red hot so we could grill the hamburgers. We played with the children out in the wide expanse of well-cared-for lawns.

At first, we did not pay attention to the cars and motorcycles pulling up and men dressed in black leather coming around us. In just a few minutes, there was a mass of men with dark and sullen expressions glaring at us. We were at the wrong place at the wrong time. We took the hibachi with briquets, just turning white, and dumped them into the creek, picked up our supplies and children, and walked as inconspicuously as possible through the throng of angry men. We were still frightened when we got home, and the idea of grilling hamburgers had left all of us. We never went back to that area, and later wondered if we had unwittingly chosen an area where drugs were being sold.

I can think of another time when I did not feel safe. This is the only time I can remember, in the many trips I took across Wyoming, that I had this kind of experience. I had been working late and headed home over the mountains after dark. I pulled up to a restaurant where I had stopped many other times. I walked into the large dining room.

There was a group sitting over to the side. They turned and stared at me with expressions that made me feel cold. I sat down, but before the waitress came with water and a menu, that voice I know so well spoke inside of me: "You need to leave this place immediately!" The command was so clear that I got up did not look over at the group sitting there watching me, went to my car, locked the doors, and headed out as quickly as possible. I didn't make any more stops until I pulled into my garage. I settled for a peanut butter sandwich and hot tea that night, just glad to be home and thankful for the Shepherd, always watching out for His sheep.

On a lighter side, one of those gifts passed on to me from my parents is the shear pleasure of cooking and entertaining in my home. Baking is at the top of the lists of my favorites. I don't think I have ever bought a pie crust. I am always on the lookout for deep-dish pie pans. I always have to make cherry pie for my grown children, but after that pie is made, I can branch out to coconut cream or apple crisp, and many times experiment with new recipes. I make mincemeat pie once a year for myself, with all kinds of chiding from my family.

Whenever I have dinner guests, I wait to put the croissant rolls in the oven until after the guests have arrived. The smell of yeast rolls baking in the oven brings pleasure that is hard to explain. There is something special about sitting around the dining room table with friends and family. I enjoy eating in restaurants, but dinners have a special intimate place of friendship in the home.

All of our family likes to cook. I have a nice sized kitchen, but when all of the family comes, they like to take part in cooking, and it becomes crowded. We take great delight in some of Paul's specialties he has brought from Wyoming. He and Craig would have to be considered chefs in their own right. Rachel makes unusual and fun things I have never heard of.

Biscuits and cream

On the McClaflin homestead, there were always some barnyard cats. Every summer I managed to adopt one or two kittens. The only criteria I used for my choice of kittens were that they had to be willing to be dressed up and enjoy riding around in the doll-sized baby buggy. Mornings and evenings, the cats would stroll out to the small shed where Mike milked the cow. I grew up taking delight in Mike's antics. He had mastered the skill of squirting the milk right into the cats' mouths as they sat there in a row. Well, almost mastered, I should say. The cats didn't seem to mind, as they would later clean themselves up and lick each other's faces until no one would have known the difference.

Those simple pleasures of growing up on a farm were the sources of many enjoyable moments in the early years of childhood.

Mike would carry the bucket of milk to the well house, where I would pour it into a cream separator. This would separate the cream and milk. Mom made butter and cottage cheese, and some of the cream was sold to the local creamery in town. It was important to wash and sanitize the separator as soon as the job was done, as the milk would sour very quickly, and then it was a slimy process, which was not pleasant.

Not all of the cream was separated from the milk, which was stored in a gallon glass jar in the refrigerator. About an inch of cream could be skimmed off the top when the milk got cold. Cooking for a hungry family and hired men alongside my mom was hard work. Getting the work done on the northern farms of Wyoming with a short growing season took the help of all the family members. I didn't realize what a privilege was afforded me until later, when cooking for large groups of people came naturally to me.

The homemade ice cream, chocolate cakes, and biscuits made with heavy cream were a regular menu in the McClaflin household. When I could no longer have heavy cream at my disposal, I had to find a whole new assortment of recipes to cook with.

I remember one Booher family reunion that was held in the mountains up near Grand Junction, Colorado. We were driving from Detroit, so we stopped in Fleming on the way and stayed with Mom and Dad Booher overnight. Dad took me out to see his new purchase, a beautiful Jersey cow. He sent me off the next morning with a quart of heavy cream. While at the family reunion, we stayed in an old trailer with an oven. I was delighted with the gift of cream, as I had not been able to make the childhood recipes for a long time.

I would get up early in order to make biscuits from the cream. One morning, I noticed one of the guests wasn't eating biscuits. When I asked him, he said he didn't care for biscuits. The next morning, I said, "Why don't you just take a bite of one of these biscuits?" He reluctantly took one of the hot biscuits off the plate. As he took a bite, his face broke out in a smile. "Oh, my goodness!" he exclaimed. I didn't have to ask him again for the duration of the reunion, as he would take several on his plate every morning.

Many years have passed since those biscuits made with pure cream right off the farm. It wouldn't do for my figure at this point, as I don't get the physical exercise I did as a young girl. I am grateful for this season of my life, writing down those cherished memories of another time.

Eating is a vital part of survival, but when one has to eat in a place where they do not feel safe, or among persons who are hostile, or even considered an enemy, it is not a pleasant experience. If a person finds themselves in constant upheaval while eating, it can affect good health, and also decreases one's appetite.

Shepherd's protection and daily provision

Ronnie gave a good analogy to his flocks of sheep in relation to this verse, "You prepare a table before me in the presence of my enemies."

"In the 23rd Psalm, it speaks of the Shepherd preparing a table before me in the presence of my enemies. I can think of an example when lambs are out in the fields. If there is a predator, they will not go near. They are not comfortable, so they don't eat well and they are always watchful and they are not at peace. As long as the predator is close by, whether it is a dog, coyote, fox, wolf, or whatever the predator might be, the sheep cannot be comfortable. The sheep doesn't have any protection except getting away from the predator and the danger they are in. As shepherds, we have to give them a table of green pastures to eat in that is safe and not infected with predators or other things that distract the sheep like flies and other nuisances for the sheep. When we put them out into a field, they need to have the peace and comfort in knowing they are not going to be molested by predators.

"Sheep have many predators. They have internal predators, and they have external parasites and predators that chew on them, like face flies, which bother them considerably. They walk around with their head down close to the ground, trying to keep the flies off of their head. Today, we have insecticides that we can use to keep the flies away from the sheep. Before insecticides were available, shepherds used to put oil on the sheep's head to keep the flies away. This would last for two or three weeks, and then they would have to re-treat the sheep."

CHAPTER 9:
You Anoint My Head With Oil, My Cup Overflows

I am humming to myself, "You never promised me a rose garden." As this song depicts, life is full of surprise and sometimes disappointment. It is easy to fall into the thought process, "If I do things right, am honest, work hard, follow the Ten Commandments, then my life will be without trial." Unfortunately, this is not usually the case.

Throughout scripture, you and I are admonished to look to God as our source of strength, and to live justly. As we stroll back through history, we can find people who lived through great difficulty, and yet they remained strong in their faith. Two of my favorite chapters in the Psalms are 37 and 91. When days seem to get hectic, or I find myself fretting, I just sit quietly and by the time I have read the last two verses of chapter 91, I am ready once more to get up and be about the Master's call.

"He will call upon me, and I will answer him; I will be with him in trouble, I will deliver him and honor him. With long life will I satisfy him and show him my salvation." Psalm 91:15-16

I can think of no moment more blessed than when one feels the touch of anointing from the Heavenly Father. It can come while strolling by a dark and cool mountain stream. It can come in the early morning hours of prayer while the hush of evening dew is still in the air. I have seen this anointing presence touch saints as they stand in the sanctuary, lifting holy hands in adoration and worship.

No other human emotion can convey with such depth the feeling of personal worth, tenderness, and consuming love that one experiences in those moments of anointing.

As a very young girl, I can remember my mother singing in the choir in the Methodist church. I grew up cherishing the old hymns. One particular melody comes to mind as I am writing today. I would be so moved by the words of this song that I would weep, sitting there next to my father, listening to my mother's beautiful lyric soprano voice.

THERE IS A BALM IN GILEAD

There is a balm in Gilead
To make the wounded whole,
There is a balm in Gilead
To save my sin sick soul.
Sometimes I feel discouraged
And I feel I can't go on,
But then the Holy Spirit revives my soul again.
If you cannot preach like Peter,
If you cannot preach like Paul,
Oh, you can tell the Love of Jesus
You can say he died for us all.

Version of old spiritual found in Washington Glass's 1854 hymn
"The Sinner's Cure"

I woke early this morning, with a song in my mind. I haven't heard it for years and don't even remember the title, but it has to do with the anointing. It is a beautiful song, penned by one who surely has experienced this very special blessing from God.

In my early morning prayer time, I reached up on the shelf for my volumes of the Psalms by Charles Spurgeon. This collection is a cherished gift from a friend from many years ago now. All day, I have brooded over how I would express this brief passage, "You anoint my head with oil, my cup runs over."

I have always been drawn to the Psalms. Many mornings in the quiet stillness before the rising of the sun, making sure all the windows are closed, I strap on my old accordion and sing praises to God. There is something that brings a portion of the divine down into the rooms of a person's home, which has come to love this Heavenly Shepherd, when they worship in song.

Throughout the Bible, we see the importance of anointing. The ceremony of anointing was used for kings and priests. Old Testament prophets were touched with a Heavenly anointing. As we read throughout the New Testament, we note the special anointing that followed the apostles.

One of the great joys of a parent is to watch their children grow into full stature and give back to humanity. Rachel falls in line as the youngest, and she has become a minister. She has an ability to teach the Bible in a way that gives insight and meaning in today's society. For the last few weeks, I have enjoyed listening to her as she has taught in the Book of Acts. I found myself once again reflecting on Stephen and the circumstances that surrounded his becoming a martyr (Acts 7:54–60).

There was a young man on the sidelines by the name of Saul, giving consent to Stephen's death. As one reads the account of Stephen in his last moments on this earth, he was not concerned with himself but prayed for those who would stone him to death:

"Lord, do not charge them with this sin." Acts 7:60

If one were to look into the face of Stephen that day, blood gushing down his body, the anointing of God's glory would have shown on his face, as it states he was full of the Holy Spirit, and he said,

"Look! I see the heavens opened and the Son of Man standing at the right hand of God," and the verse says, he fell asleep. (Acts 7:56) What a homecoming it must have been on that day Stephen came home to his maker.

Saul was a religious man, doing what he thought was right. He was persecuting the church. Many saints saw their death because of Saul. What a powerful story of conversion we see in the life of Saul, who was later, renamed Paul in Acts chapter 9. Because of his devotion to God, Paul would later make a pivotal point in propagating Christianity throughout the world.

I find myself poring over the epistles written by the Apostle Paul. Through the years, the words penned have empowered my life. I am brought to tears as I realize the last years of his life were in a prison cell. At times, he would ask his friends to bring him a coat, as he was cold. As one follows the life of Paul, it is apparent an anointing of God's spirit was like a mantle over him. To see the transformation of thought from chapters 7 and 8 of Romans has been a flagstone in my personal life. The challenge to press on to a higher place in God gives humanity a hope and future. Paul's death came when he was beheaded for his testimony for Jesus Christ. I am sure that at Paul's homecoming, next to the Shepherd of Heaven, Stephen stood with arms open wide, ready to receive him.

The Bible in its entirety is my highest treasure. I have carried a reference study Bible in my traveling bag for many years. I left my first edition, marked throughout with scriptures that became a road map in my own life's journey, in Russia with a new convert while working on a short term teaching assignment at Saratov University. I began again with an NIV translation, marked it up, and left it with my secretary Dori, who had not only been my faithful comrade in the work place at the UW Extension office, but a cherished friend for many years.

So once again, I sit in this early morning, as the dew lifts off of the greenery close to my sunroom window, with another reference study Bible. My mind is full and the thoughts come rapidly to me.

On my bedroom wall in front of my bed is a picture I have carried with me for many years. It is a little shepherd girl that was given to me by a lady named Carolyn Haley. When she came with the picture, she explained it was something she had treasured, but the Lord told her she should give it away. So when our family was moving from a congregation we had cherished for many years, she came with the picture. How could she know at that time what a comfort this picture would bring to me?

This afternoon, I took it off the wall and brought it into the office to study one more time. As I study this little shepherd girl, my prayer is that I will have the courage to write about this anointing of oil that begins at the top of the head and flows on down to the feet, forever changing one's destiny and knowledge of God.

Early and late as I look at the picture on the bedroom wall, I find myself studying the girl, dressed in blue, watching over the flock of sheep on a hot summer afternoon. It is a simple frock she wears with a well-worn straw hat to protect her from the heat. She is a little shepherd girl who has been instructed by the Shepherd to care for the sheep.

How many times has the soft voice of the Shepherd encouraged me to watch for the little lambs in the form of children, touch an elderly person's hand, or hug a crying mother?

I am trying to remember when I first felt this anointing from God's hand on my life. Some of the first recollections would be when I was riding my horse out in the Wyoming prairies, alone with my thoughts, and they were often on God. I would look up into the billowing clouds in the sky and feel his presence in such a way that my soul and spirit would overflow with a sense of love being poured out as an anointing of oil.

Our family attended a small church in my hometown of Powell. The pastor's wife was such a tiny little thing. I think she wore size three shoes. I would always sit with her. There was an old altar that stretched out across the front of the church. After service I would go and spend long periods of time praying. She would kneel down beside me and never leave me. So many times as I prayed next to this saint, I would feel the presence of God's anointing. The congregation called them Brother and Sister Thiemann, and I knew they both loved me dearly. At times I would feel such joy; I cannot describe it in words. At other times as this anointing would come to me, I would have deep sorrow as I sought God. Travailing in prayer is rarely mentioned today, but in those years as a young child, I truly believe that is when God was teaching me to seek Him in my times of prayer at the altar and out riding my horse in a solitary sanctuary of prayer on the hills and valleys at the crest of the Rockies.

A foundation was laid in those young childhood years that has served me well. Life has brought its hardship. At times, I have been bewildered at the obstacles I have faced. But I could never get away from the memories of the depth of love I felt from God in those times of quiet anointing, when He would fill my heart as a cup running over, leaving me with a sense of being loved, which nothing on earth could match. Whenever I would begin to swerve off the path that would take me away from this

Shepherd of Heaven, I would have such a sense of loss that I would run back into His arms.

Those early years of my life, learning about the love God had for me personally, has created within me a passion for sharing the knowledge of this wonderful Shepherd with young children.

When our three children were very young, the church began a bus ministry. We would visit homes in the area, and on Sunday mornings would pick up the children. Sometimes they would still be in pajamas, and I am sure many of them had not had breakfast yet. Many of these children had never been in church. Not everyone in the congregation was excited about these little ruffians. Many times, there would only be two or three of us ministering to about a hundred children. I was young, inexperienced, and had a scarce supply of teaching materials. There were times after a Sunday morning I would be completely spent.

One morning at home when my own children were playing, I was praying about how I could teach those scruffy little children. The creative mind kicked in. My first puppets were a choir of five, made from papier mâché. I cut my broom handle into five pieces, formed strange and goofy heads, painted them; designed choir robes, and entered into a world of seeing God through the lens of young children. From that point, our children's church had lions, dogs, and human faces of many sorts. The ugliest puppet was Pink Baby, and of course, it was the favorite of the children

When I was a young child, I would line my dolls up on the bed and care for them. I always wanted to be a mother, so my heart was blessed with our son Craig and daughters, Shana and Rachel. When the bus ministry started, the demands that came with it were overwhelming and exhausting. It didn't take long for the realization to unfold within me of the faces of these children. I not only loved my own children, in fact I loved all children. Throughout the week, I would be inspired to create materials made from everyday items around the home to enhance the Sunday morning Bible stories.

Craig became involved with the puppets and was one of my staunchest supporters when he was six years old. The experiences with those groups of children that came on buses every Sunday morning are a long-ago memory, but everywhere I go I see the faces of children, and I am blessed.

Looking back on that time, I pray that those little children grew up to know the Heavenly Shepherd.

Our church started a school, which was named Fairlane Christian School in the Detroit area. I have many rich memories of the years I taught there. One specific time comes to mind as I write this portion on the anointing. The prayers began in a classroom, and the intensity of seeking God spread throughout the school. This kind of moving of God's spirit cannot be orchestrated; it is a divine and sovereign anointing He pours out on those seeking Him with all their hearts. As we prayed with the students, it was apparent that even very small children were being anointed as their faces took on a radiance that was from Heaven. Rachel and Shana were in the fifth and sixth grade at the time. As the children were gathered around praying, some of them stood and would preach to the others. As Rachel stood and began to preach, I just wept, knowing that the words she spoke had to come from a special anointing that would follow her throughout her life.

The children that experienced that powerful move of God in those days of prayer were forever changed. I would pray to God that all children would find themselves in a place where they could experience that kind of anointing while still young.

The anointing that is spoken of in the Psalms is what brings healing to the deepest wound. The oil of the Holy Spirit is what propels man into greatness, as witnessed in the life of Stephen the martyr and the Apostle Paul. God longs to pour out this same anointing on today's men and women and children, if they will only seek him with all their hearts.

> *"For I know the thoughts that I think toward you, says the Lord,*
> *thoughts of peace and not of evil, to give you a future and a hope.*
> *Then you will call upon Me and go and pray to Me,*
> *and I will listen to you. And you will*
> *seek Me and find Me, when you search for Me*
> *with all your heart." Jeremiah 29:11–14 NKJV*

God's voice comes to us in numerous ways. Many times the oil of anointing will come in the quiet of nature. I traveled a good deal while I worked for the university, so when I had the privilege of being home in Shell for the weekend, I was content and full of peace. I made sure I had gotten the grocery items needed so I wouldn't have to go to town. I attended church on Sunday, but then I enjoyed my home with the pets.

One blustery spring morning, I was enjoying a cup of coffee sitting out on the deck. It wasn't unusual to see massive eagles flying up next to the mountainside where my home was situated. As I sat there relishing the quiet, I saw a huge eagle begin to circle around just out in front of the deck. The wingspread was enormous. My eyes were transfixed on this majestic bird. With each circle, the eagle would be propelled up higher into the clouds. In just a matter of moments, I could no longer see the eagle. I sat there stunned at what I had just witnessed. I couldn't help but think that is just what it's like when we allow the Holy Spirit to anoint us with His oil. We truly are taken to a place in the divine where we are so full of God's glory and magnificence that our cup runs over with His presence.

Old barns and shepherds

There is something nostalgic about old barns no longer in use. For those of us growing up on farms or ranches, the barns were a place of work and necessity to protect the livestock. Our father did a great deal of work in building those old sheep sheds on the McClaflin homestead. When I go home to visit Mom, I always find time to slip out of the house alone and go out and walk through the barnyard and slip into the old lambing sheds.

They are long barns with dirt floors and a few lambing pens up next to the walls. It is silent as I walk down through the long shed. The only sounds I can hear are a few birds fluttering up in the rafters.

After I grew up, I always felt like I was missing out on something during the lambing season, knowing I was not able to see the little lambs frolicking out in the barnyard, feeding the bum lambs, or hearing my parents' stories of the sheep.

The men out on the homesteads became close comrades in the farming adventures. They probably learned as much from the mistakes they made as the textbook knowledge they learned in those evening classes that were given to the WWII veteran farmers early on to assist them in developing the skills of irrigation farming.

Such was the case with the families who raised sheep. My Dad and Lloyd Snider shared farm equipment, worked along together, and checked in with each other almost on a daily basis. The Sniders lived just around the corner up on the hill. The UW Agriculture Agents were regular visitors on the homestead farms, working with homesteaders and helping them with the many farming questions.

Lloyd and Dad were not only working partners, but the dearest of friends. I would characterize both of them as having Shepherd's hearts, as they both cared for their flocks of sheep. Early on after growing up, when going home, I would go to the sheep sheds with my Dad. Hopefully, if I could go home while there were still ewes with their lambs out in the barnyard, I would hear the most delightful stories. Daddy had names for many of the barnyard sheep. While working with the sheep day after day, he would observe the different temperaments and personalities. He used to tell the local pastor the sheep reminded him of congregations of people.

Looking back now on those growing-up years, if I would have had an inkling that I would someday be trying to remember the everyday goings on out in the barnyard, I hope I would have had the presence of mind to keep a journal about the day-to-day tasks that were so commonplace during that time. On a scale of animal intelligence, the sheep is not ranked at the top. In fact, sheep require a great deal of care. They are defenseless to protect themselves.

It is interesting that throughout the Bible, man is likened to sheep. Of course, sheep were part of everyday life in those times, but is there deeper meaning in the similarities? A picture in reference to a story often taught in Sunday school is about the ninety-nine sheep in the fold:

> *"Suppose one of you has a hundred sheep and loses one of them. Does he not leave the ninety-nine in the open country and go after the lost sheep until he finds it? And when he finds it, he joyfully puts it on his shoulders and goes home." Luke 15:3–5*

From a shepherd girl's reflection, I would see that the sheep have all been directed back into the pens for the night for protection. As the shepherd counts, he discovers he is missing one small lamb. He secures the latch on the gate and goes back out into the hills, although he is weary from a long hot day of herding the flock. He looks desperately as the sun sets to the west. In the distance, he hears the bleating of the frightened little lamb. He rushes down the rocky cliffs and takes into his arms the little lamb that has been stuck in a crevice of the rock. The lamb nestles down into the arms of the shepherd, as he knows he is safe. As the last rays of light pass over the horizon, the shepherd is seen coming back to the enclosed pen holding the lamb. There is no bleating of this lamb now, as he knows he is coming home.

> *"I am the good shepherd; I know my sheep and my sheep know me; just as the Father knows me and I know the Father, and I lay down my life for the sheep." John 10:14 & 15*

Many years later, after my father had been in Heaven for a number of years, I returned to Wyoming to work with the UW Extension. I was able to see Lloyd Snider once in a while, which was always a pleasure, because it seemed he had a fragrance of life like my Dad possessed. The 4-H program had been such a vital part of the McClaflin family, so I felt I wanted to give back to this youth organization. Summers were filled with many activities in preparation for the county and state fairs. Since our county fair was backed up to the state fair, getting all the exhibits labeled and prepared to transport in just a few days was a big task. After the first day of judging, I spent most of the week in the 4-H barn. Those late summer afternoons in a cement block building with a metal roof were like being in a cooker.

By Thursday, I felt like a limp and wilted piece of lettuce. My goal every year was to have the state fair exhibits labeled and ready to be boxed up before Thursday, which was sheep judging day at the Big Horn County Fair. The day began early, as the judging would go on into the evening. After sheep judging, there was a contest called the "Sheep Lead." It was sponsored by sheep producers, with the intent of encouraging people to sew with wool. I had been asked to model a wool suit I had made. The late afternoon was sweltering and I was so busy, I didn't feel like putting on a wool suit, but I wanted to support what the wool growers were doing, so I agreed to take part in the contest.

The Big Horn County Fair is a community project. Compared to other counties, it was not so big in size, but I felt it was so down-home. There were large trees that gave shade for the many activities throughout the week. It took a concerted effort on the whole community to conduct the fair.

One particular year that sticks out in my mind was the year I sat and watched the sheep judging with the fair manager, John Haley. By Thursday, my feet and legs ached, so I would wear the most comfortable tennis shoes I had, and hopefully I would be able to find a place to sit down as I watched the judging. I had called my mother early, asking her to come over to the Sheep Lead contest. No, actually I was tearfully begging her to come. I was so weary, and melancholy was moving in fast, I just didn't want to walk around in the Sheep Lead without her sitting up there in the bleachers.

In the afternoon, I came out of the 4-H exhibit hall and found a seat under one of the big trees. I was watching one of the classes of sheep being judged, when John Haley saw me and came over and sat down. He looked exhausted. I was tired, but I don't think my fatigue came close to his. As he sat there, he began to talk about my Dad. I looked at him; his face was red; and I could tell he was fighting back tears, as well as me. Oh dear, I wanted to hear what he said, so I listened carefully, as the ache in my chest increased. "Pat, I remember Wallace and Lloyd Snider years ago when they came to judge the sheep contest at our fair. We started early in the morning, and the judging would go into the night. After the long day of judging, I would see your Dad over there in the sheep barn with 4-H'ers, talking to them individually, telling them what they could do the next year to improve their judging skills."

There are times one just wants to roll the clock of time back, but we can't do that, can we? He got up and walked away. After a while he came back again, telling me how much he respected my Dad and just how much he missed him.

After a while I had to go back into the hot exhibit hall and keep working. I kept going to the back door, looking for my mom's car. She didn't want to drive by herself, so she had Felix Hoff come with her. Bessie had died several years earlier of a stroke. The Hoffs were our close family friends, so he would have understood my sadness on sheep judging day. When I saw them, I walked out; just needing a hug, not wanting her to know how much my heart ached on that day.

Those times of working at fairs are behind me now. I don't know if I could keep up with that pace of work anymore. I am glad for those years of working with the 4-H program again, but it is so good to be here in Michigan with the grandchildren. My two granddaughters are so proud of the 4-H dresses they made this year. We already have plans for sewing with wool next year. I am going to go to the Extension office this fall and teach a class on tailoring and sewing with wool. Maybe, just maybe, I can help some young child learn a skill in a 4-H project so someday in the future they can look back on a little grandma-type person who loved young people.

4-H Sewing Project

It was August and the fair would be in just a few days. The 4-H sewing projects had been completed and judged. Anna and Elizabeth, my twin granddaughters of twelve, had mentioned last winter they wanted to do some sewing for competition. No moss grew under my feet, as I quickly went to Sandy and Craig and asked if I could be the girls' 4-H sewing leader.

I tend to wear rose-colored glasses at crucial and pivotal points of life. The glasses came off quickly as the sewing projects began. My plan was to have regular meetings, allowing the girls time to sew with ease, no deadlines to be met, just a wonderful relaxing time with Grandma. If you are a parent of preteens, I can hear you laughing already. You know the score by now. How to fit one more activity into a household of five children would be a leap of faith. Craig and Sandy have two teenage boys, the twin girls are preteen, and then comes Reagan, our young man ready for kindergarten.

There were many special moments with those two beautiful girls, but there were also long hours of instruction as I sat next to them, teaching them the skills of sewing I had learned so many years ago from my mother and Edith Anderson, Park County Home Economist.

I would describe Edith and Niles Anderson as salt of the earth kinds of people. She passed away many years ago, but there have been many times I wished I could have gone to her and told her the profound impact she had on my life, as she would become one of my life's heroes. When I came back to Wyoming and took a position with the UW Extension as a county agent, I came to realize just how incredible that couple was.

Edith had salt-and-pepper hair, braided and neatly coiled in a bun at the back of her neck. She walked with a cane, but that didn't slow her down. She was a woman with a soft-spoken voice that carried with it wisdom of experience and Godly character. Niles worked alongside his wife, always ready to encourage and inspire young people.

Edith would give regular sewing classes to the 4-H leaders. I remember the day she taught me how to make bound button holes for my wool suit. She came to our home to personally examine the wedding dress I was designing for myself. So many memories come to mind of so long ago of a gentle, quiet couple that inscribed on my heart that I was special.

Granddaughters Anna and Elizabeth with 4-H
blue ribbons at Jackson County Fair

I met Sandy and the girls in the parking lot of Jackson County Fairgrounds on Saturday morning. Many years of working at the county and state fairs in Wyoming were behind me. I wasn't going to be a sewing judge, or have to attend to the many tasks of running 4-H activities at a fair. I was Grandma, and I would stand back with their mother and watch, as the girls entered into a new experience of interview judging. They were nervous. Would they remember what they were supposed to say? Would the judge be nice? Would she like their dresses?

When it was time for each of the girls to step before the judge, holding the dress they had worked on so carefully, it was as if Sandy and I were the only parents in the universe, as we watched both of them explain in detail what they had done and why. I could tell she was a good judge; she knew her stuff. They both received blue ribbons, and we were all so proud of the accomplishment of the reward of sewing with excellence.

Their father went on Saturday, so the girls could show their Papa the dresses on display in the showcase in the 4-H exhibit hall. Dads can be described as the icing on the cake, as the girls will long remember the look of pride on his face, just as I remember my father's face.

County fair was always a big week for the McClaflin family. Not only were my brothers and I involved with 4-H exhibits, but Mom and Dad invested many years with the youth of Park County in making the fair possible as they worked along with many other volunteers.

The fine-tuned senses of being a child were instilled in the evenings after the judging contests were complete, as the smells of cotton candy and the music from the big merry-go-round would summon us. The tilt-a-whirl was my favorite, as I liked the speed and pressure of going round and round.

The fast pace of today's world is often likened to being on a merry-go-round with speed picking up as the years go by, until we can no longer see the faces of those standing by, watching the colorful horses moving in a circle of motion.

I have lighted on the ground and look back at that busy time of sewing with my granddaughters, knowing the deadline was coming up shortly, but the look on their faces holding up the blue ribbons was worth every weary moment working into the late-night hours.

This morning I am back in my upstairs office, sitting before my computer, penning down the thoughts going so deep inside of me now. I have pulled out the Wyoming map, well worn with years. I have taped pictures of the Shell Canyon above me on the bookshelves. I wish I could drive up into the canyon this morning, but I need to write, and I now live in Michigan.

Shell Creek on west side of
Big Horn Mountain range in Wyoming

The alternate South Highway 14 is kept open throughout the year for travelers going over the Big Horn Mountains. Many times, coming home from a long week at the university or returning from several days of judging at adjoining county fairs, I would be weary. The scenery was beautiful, and I always enjoyed it. But in those years, I would be counting off the miles by increments, wanting to get home and walk into the house sitting up on the hill, looking right into the canyon. I knew I would be home soon when I reached the west side of the mountain range and started down the switchbacks. If it was late in the summer during fair time, as I dropped in elevation with each turn of the highway, I knew I would be met with a hot blast of air as I reached the valley floor. When I had passed the Shell falls, I would open my window, knowing I would soon be able to hear the falling of water down the mountain ravine and smell the mist coming up from the stream running along side the road. I am grateful for every day I lived in my home in Shell, Wyoming, as the view was breathtaking.

It is hard to be involved with grandchildren on a daily basis long distance, so in this season of my life, I live near them, where I can see their

Patricia McClaflin Booher

faces, hear them laugh, give them a hug when they cry. The bonus for me is the majestic trees outside my window and trips to Lake Michigan.

This morning, as I have found my quiet place of solitude that allows me to write, I find myself looking closely at the topographic map of the Big Horn Mountain range. Shell is only a small hamlet, so one has to look carefully to find her nestled right at the foot of the mountain range.

There were many times when the heat seemed to drain me of strength; after a long day of work, I would slip up to the Shell Falls and be rejuvenated by the still pools of quiet. I went back through my files this morning and pulled out a poem I had written that spring while recovering from back surgery.

DEEP CALLS TO DEEP

The winter time of the soul,
Brings a heaviness of Spirit,
It brings loneliness and despair.
Like a heavy snow on a waterfall,
Is the weight of this season.
But out of the deep dark, and cold pools of winter,
Comes a new life and joy.
And after a season of discipline comes spring!

Patricia, April, 1994

There is a scripture in Psalm 42 that has drawn me into its words for many years now. I have asked many times, of those more learned than myself, the meaning of this passage, never finding a reply that seemed to satisfy my desire to know the depth of meaning. I have taken this passage out of context, as I reflect upon it at this point of my journey:

"Deep calls to deep in the roar of your waterfalls;
all your waves and breakers have swept over me." Psalm 42:7

The poem I penned was written during the early thaw when the Shell Falls were still encased with snow and ice. It made for a spectacular picture, as one would gaze down into the ravine seeing the deep and clear viridian blue, icy cold water. As I stood on the small veranda reaching out over the granite boulders, encased with tall pines giving off an evergreen scent, enhanced by the rays of moisture, calmness would come over my spirit.

Growing up on a homestead afforded the luxury of quiet. There were no radios blasting, earphones, or cell phones to invade this sanctuary of solitude as I worked out in the bean field, hoeing weeds, or walked in the pasture with the sheep flock. I remember as a very young child an awareness of God, and I loved him. Looking out over the mountain range, seeing the magnificent western sunset, could only reinforce faith in a Creator of Heaven and Earth.

Farming, gardening, and childhood

Have you ever taken the time to look at another person's hands, or even yours, for that matter? Hands speak volumes about a person. Even though, at this time in my life's journey, I live in the city, down inside of me is a farm girl. I keep several pairs of garden gloves right by the back door, but often when I go out to check the flowers and vegetables, I find myself down on the ground, digging around in the soil bare handed. I like the feel of the cool, rich dirt running through my fingers. How often as a child did I see my mother and father do the same thing out on the farm they loved so well. But alas, I now live in the city, so I make sure to check my hands before leaving the garden for soil that has been embedded under my fingernails.

I cannot say I save money by planting a garden every spring, but the pure pleasure I receive every morning in checking the small garden cannot be measured in currency.

Gardening is such a quiet, simple task, and yet for those of us who have this hobby, we know the importance of the tranquility of spirit that comes with seeing the first buds of spring popping out on the tilled rich soil.

This was going to be a special year for gardening. I knew I would be confined to my upstairs office writing, so I gave special effort in buying many mature plants that would produce vegetables early in the summer. The garden would become my regrouping five-minute break away from staring at the computer.

Every year, I add one or two ceramic pots to my deck. I arrange the color wheel arrangement of deep purple, fuchsia, a touch of lemon yellow, and of course white flowers to different sizes and heights of unusual, artistic planters.

I am fond of the deer that roam throughout the neighborhood, but this summer they have taken more than their share of my garden. I had paid an extra amount for fine specimens of cucumber and tomato plants. My morning habit was to check the small green tomatoes and the little cucumbers that were already taking form. I do believe the simple pleasures of life often bring the deepest satisfaction. One morning I went out, and to my great dismay, the cucumber plants had been eaten down to the ground. The small green tomatoes with bright yellow blossoms were gone, and only barren stubs stuck up from the ground. I stopped my morning schedule and went directly to the local hardware store. I didn't want to get electric shockers, so I decided on special spray that was to discourage the deer. I sprayed all the plants in the yard, including the flowers on the deck, just in case those deer decided to come up the wooden stairs and invade my lovely ceramic pots of flowers. By now, I was feeling some guilt, as this whole procedure was biting into scheduled time for writing.

The next morning, when I began my walk through the yard, I was met with such a horrible smell, I found myself gagging. I couldn't open my office window, as the aroma lifted up to the second story of my home. This went on for several days. The deer didn't come around, but I wondered how long this dreadful smell would last.

Life settled down, and weeks went by with no more invasions, and then it happened again. I tried other deterrents that friends said would work for sure. I did manage to get a few cucumbers about two inches long, and three tomatoes from my garden. I finally gave up and went down to the farmer's market, which turned out to be an enjoyable break from writing. Michigan has wonderful garden farms, so I am happy to support these hard-working folks, and I have grown to enjoy visiting with the farmers on a regular basis.

On Friday mornings Shana brings the three youngest grandsons to my home for a preschool of sorts. It is wishful thinking, but we try and get a few minutes in the sunroom to drink a warm cup of tea while the young ones watch their favorite cartoons. Maximus is very quick and much smarter then his grandma and auntie. When he was in his toddler stage, we shut the French doors and confined him with us in the sunroom. He would look longingly at the older boys through the glass, but alas we would have a few cherished moments to quickly share the whole week of highlights. One day while I was cleaning up with glass cleaner in my hand, I saw the handprints of Maximus on the French doors. I got down on my knees and studied the pudgy little prints of that precious little boy, and decided I could clean on another day, as it brought such delight to my heart as I thought of him.

A few months ago, I took a pause in my busy schedule and flew home to see Mom. She had not been feeling well, and I just felt I needed to see her. My daughter Rachel, Mitch, and the boys came along and we converged on the homestead. Mike and Linda had scheduled a flight on the same weekend, and Pam and Wayne spent a good deal of time with us. It is not often that the whole family gets to sit around the old farm table, so it was a special time.

While there, Mom taught Rachel how to knit. Mitch and Rachel both took many pictures of the events of the weekend. A few days after we came home, Rachel gave me a small picture book she had compiled with a computer program she has. It was such a precious little book of memories. I was just fine until I turned to the pages with pictures of my mother's hands, and then I cried.

Each of us has the ability to strike out with our hands in anger, or give a touch that brings solace and comfort to another. I found often in the classroom when a student was unsettled, I could gently place my hand on his or her shoulder and it would usually bring calm to the troubled child.

> *Because Your loving kindness is better than life,*
> *My lips shall praise You.*
> *Thus I will bless you while I live;*
> *I will lift up my hands in Your name.*
> *Because You have been my help,*
> *Therefore in the shadow of Your wings I will rejoice.*
> *My soul follows close behind You;*
> *Your right hand upholds me. Psalm 63: 3, 4, 7 & 8*

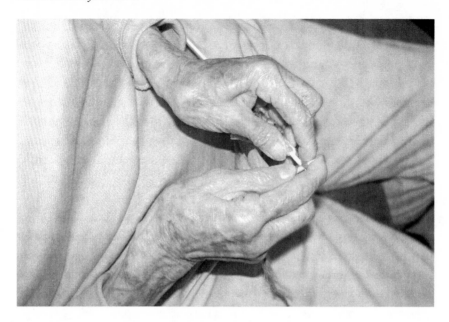

Edna Mae McClaflin showing granddaughter,
Rachel Ross how to knit

Mom has tiny hands and feet, but that did not stop her from working alongside Daddy all those years. The homesteaders planted large gardens from the very beginning. In those early years, we ate a lot of venison. The war veterans were starting a new life out on the prairies, sharing farm equipment, and working alongside each other. Families lived very frugally, but I think they all considered themselves very rich.

Summers were spent caring for the garden and then canning and freezing the produce. As I have grown older, I have often wished I had paid closer attention to Mom's gardening knowledge. I spent a lot of time out in the garden pulling weeds, but if I was working alongside Mom, I was chattering away like young children do, but I think that was important too. We didn't have air conditioning, so late-summer days in the kitchen canning hundreds of quarts of food was hot and tiring. The reward for the hard work was a great sense of accomplishment, as we looked at the jars of fruits and vegetables sitting on the shelves out in the well house. I still bring home Mom's sweet pickles, packed away in the luggage, always hoping the jars don't get broken. I can't seem to make the family's favorite potato salad without those special pickles.

Life on those farms required hard work throughout the year. Summers were filled with planting, irrigating, and harvesting crops. Caring for livestock was a day-by-day task. Daddy's hands reflected the labor he gladly did for his family. One fall day, while working on the combine out in the shop, preparing for harvest, Daddy had a terrible accident. A metal bar came loose, flew up, and hit the under part of his lower arm. The arm was so badly broken and bruised that setting it in a cast had to be postponed for days. As was the custom of those homestead men, they quickly regrouped, came with combines, and harvested the McClaflin crops.

There were complications with the arm. Infection set in where the cast rubbed on bruised skin. Because it was a compound fracture with splintering, healing came slowly. As the arm healed, the fingers in his left hand drew down, so that for the rest of his life, he couldn't straighten out his hand. While out in the sheep barns in frigid January mornings, his hand would ache from the cold.

I knew that his hand hurt at times, but I never gave much thought to the fact that his hand was crippled; he was my Dad, and I loved his hard-working, calloused hands. Later in his life he made a comment about his hand, indicating he was a bit embarrassed. I was surprised, because it would never have occurred to me he felt that way.

Throughout scripture, hands have been used symbolically to indicate God's protection and caring. The plan of salvation of mankind from the dawning of the ages would require a sacrifice. One day, when I stand before Christ, what an honor it will be to see His face, this Shepherd who has walked me throughout life, with His hand in mine. When I can bring my eyes from the glory of radiance of the Great Shepherd's face, there will be a desire to look at His hands.

CHAPTER 10:

SURELY GOODNESS AND MERCY

When the movie "The Passion" came to theaters in our city, I knew I needed to go. Groups of the congregation went during the week, but Craig said he wanted to take me, so I waited till Saturday afternoon to go with him. I don't think there was an empty seat left in the auditorium. Early into the movie, I put my head down, and before the movie was even to the halfway point, I couldn't hold the tears back. I was relieved that I had waited to go with Craig. Many times when I pray for him, I call him the "Mighty Oak," as he is steady and strong and has a great sense of justice. When the nails were being pounded into the hands of Christ, I felt sick at my stomach, and my eyes were shut tightly. When the movie was over, the theater was totally silent. Everyone sat in their seats for a time, and then one by one, people began to stand up. Groups of people huddled together by the sides of the rows with a hushed reverence. For those of us who know this Shepherd of Heaven in a personal way, even as graphic as the movie was, the horror of Christ dying on a cross could never be depicted in its magnitude on film.

God's plan was to have His son come to earth and walk among men. The thing that is amazing to me is the grace and mercy this Son of God has poured over me all of my life, and to think He loves all of His creation with this same devotion, I cannot fathom.

There is a place for God in the heart of every person. Man searches here and there throughout the earth, longing for peace and a place of value and hope for the future.

It is God's desire that man would come to the awareness of how this Lord of Heaven has always come alongside each of us.

When I think of the mercy that describes God, I know a small measure of this character He possesses, and yet I have walked with this Shepherd for a lifetime. As I read carefully over scriptures that relate to how watchmen have been stationed on the ramparts looking over mankind, I can't help but think about my own family.

Many years ago, I was reading a passage, *"So be not afraid, for I am with you; I will bring your children from the east and gather you from the west."* Isaiah 43.5

I knew this referred to the children of Israel, but when I read those words on that morning, it was as if the Spirit of God was quickened within me. At that time, Shana lived on the West Coast, I lived in Wyoming, Rachel lived on the East Coast, and Craig and his family lived in Michigan. Years passed, and one day I remembered that verse as I looked around a holiday table, with all my family that now lives in the same community in Michigan. To my great delight on a Sunday morning, I will see all three of my children and their families file in to church and take a place of servanthood in serving God.

My grandchildren have not come to me personally to ask who my favorite is, but I have heard from their parents, conversations that they have overheard. Each of them thinks they are my favorite, but actually each one of them finds that place in my heart. The Bible speaks of children as a heritage from the Lord:

> *"Sons are a heritage from the Lord, children a reward from him."*
> Psalm 127:3

With blessing comes responsibility, as I am well aware. The greatest role a grandparent can play in a family is to be a Godly watchman on the tower. Just as in days of old when Isaiah penned the words:

> *"I have posted watchmen on your walls, O Jerusalem; they will never be silent day or night. You, who call on the Lord, give*

yourselves no rest." Isaiah 62:6

From the time Craig was a young child, it was apparent that he had been blessed with a sense of justice and could retain volumes of information about history. His bedroom became a replica of historical events. Even now, he has a hobby of painting miniatures of soldiers in battle uniform. I had gone back to college after the children were all in school. One semester, I took a required history class from a Professor Wittke. I couldn't write notes fast enough; the tests were a bear; but he made Europe come alive.

Each week, we were given fifty locations that were to be found, down to the pinpoint on historical maps. This particular assignment would take hours, so I soon brought Craig into the equation. There were many nights we stayed up late, poring over old documents. When it came time for tests, Craig became my tutor. He would grill me and grill me, and at last I did pass the class. Even with the work required, I soon realized that sitting under this man's instruction was a great privilege. If situations availed themselves, I would take Craig to college with me to hear this professor's lectures. Craig would later take classes from him as he was training to become a history teacher. He saw great potential in Craig, and when it was time for him to retire, he gave my son some of his special books.

For several weeks, Craig and Rachel have been teaching a class on church history. It blesses my heart as I watch them together bringing history to present day and helping each of us in the class to understand the impact of Christ coming to this earth, dying, and being resurrected so that you and I can have life, and that more abundantly.

As one studies history, what becomes apparent is that there is really nothing in life concerning man and his condition that is new. We have a fallen nature, and we need a Savior. Christ knew when He came to this earth that He would have to die for the sins of man, and yet He was willing to leave Heaven and be born in a lowly manger. Day after day, He invested Himself into His twelve disciples, realizing along the journey they just didn't get it, yet He demonstrated mercy and grace to them time and again.

A picture often seen in a church setting is where Jesus is sitting on a hill looking down over Jerusalem, weeping with a heavy heart, as He knows what will be facing them, and they go on in spiritual darkness.

*"O Jerusalem, Jerusalem, you who kill the prophets and stone
those sent to you, how often I have longed to gather your children
together as a hen gathers her chicks under her wings, but you
were not willing!" Luke 13:34*

God sent His son to earth, knowing He would die for the sins of the world. My heart grieves for families when they lose a child. I cannot even fathom the sacrifice God made for you and I, knowing His son, the Great Shepherd of Heaven, would suffer on a cross so our sins could be forgiven. After He was resurrected, He walked together with the disciples for a brief time. He promised He would send a comforter, and in Acts chapter 1, we are told how the Holy Spirit would come and dwell within us.

How often as I read these verses, my mind goes back once again to those lambys out in the sheep shed on cold winter mornings. We did the best we could with the bum lambs, but it wasn't as good as having a ewe constantly watching out for her newborn. Some mornings, when I came to the barn with my heavy load of milk bottles, there would be a lamb sick with scours lying off in the straw. I would feed the rest of the lambs, and then go over and pick up the sick one. Many times, the lamb's wool would be soiled, but I didn't care about that as I would gently pick the little one up in my arms and hold its head up by my chest and help it drink. I couldn't save all the lambs, but I do think even a sick little orphan lamb is given hope when tender hands and loving prayers are said over them.

Reading over this 23rd Psalm, I am reminded once again that the Shepherd depicted here walks through every season of life with man. He wants to pour his mercy and grace over every situation, but how often we are like that stubborn old ewe who wants to run off through the fence and get into trouble, many times taking other foolish followers with her. Scriptures tells us that we are forever on the mind of the Lord. He wants to come alongside each of us, as it says so clearly in Psalm 23:

"Surely goodness and mercy shall follow me, all the days of my life."
Psalm 23:6

Those years of teaching in the classroom at Fairlane Christian School in the Detroit area were blessed. For a time, Valerie Somjak and I were the administrators and teachers for the preschool. Observing and loving those young children day after day always gave me a sense of awe, knowing God had designed each of them with unique personalities and gifts.

I felt like I had come home to a lifelong dream in those years while teaching junior high and high school. I was a hands-on teacher. Some of my creative techniques of teaching were a great success. Some lesson plans needed refining, but teaching invigorated me, and I always was challenged to grow along with the students.

As one looks back on their own life's journey, it is interesting to note how all of life's experiences build layers of a foundation. Even the tragic parts of life can be used for goodness if the Heavenly Shepherd is allowed to bring healing and restoration.

My children were all in school when I returned to finish my college degree. I remember that first morning, walking across the campus of Eastern Michigan University. I was full of joy as I was finally able to see that childhood dream of one day being a teacher beginning to become a reality.

God's hand was on my life as He directed me toward the degrees I would pursue. The minor in Child Development and Administration under the direction of Dr. Judy Williston and Dr. Phyllis Young was nothing short of incredible.

I would walk through the chambers on the university campus with my head held high, and in the classroom I sat in the front row like a sponge with a thirst for knowledge. I don't recall ever turning in an assignment late. At times, I felt a bit sorry for those students right out of high school. Their youth was an advantage, but the passion that drove me gave me strength of endurance.

By the time I had finished my MS degree in Family and Child Development; my education had led me from prenatal through the complete life cycle. The winter semester my Grandmother Hannah died, I was taking a course entitled "Middle to Later Years," taught by Dr. Duane Laws. From the time I was a very young child, I had an innate sense of the importance of grandparents, so this course was very meaningful to me. One evening, I asked Dr. Laws why this particular course was required, and he replied, "If it wasn't required, students wouldn't take it." I have reflected many times on what I learned that winter from him. He heightened my awareness of the importance of the later stages of life. It also validated my belief in the vital role grandparents can play in building resilient traits in the younger generation.

Later when I worked with UW Extension and would be involved in nutrition education, I would fondly think of my professor, Dr. Elaine Found, who became a role model of teaching with excellence, as her extensive knowledge of nutrition and research was commendable. Dr. Betty Barber challenged the fiber of my foundation, and for that I am grateful. And on and on I could go, with those professors who invested so much into me.

A lover of trees and a passion for teaching

Growing up on a homestead in the northern part of Wyoming gave me an appreciation for trees. In those early years of farming, with nothing in view but sagebrush and cactus, the young farmers all planted trees. The brutal winters and unrelenting winds took a heavy toll on their endeavors. Mike and I would longingly look at the small saplings out in the windbreak and wonder if they would ever be tall enough to allow us to build a tree house during our growing-up years.

Later when I had my own children, we moved to Michigan, where there are magnificent forests of trees everywhere. And now as I am in my grand parenting years, I look at trees and marvel at their beauty. I have the desk in my office parallel to the double windows so I can see the mighty evergreen just outside the window.

When I need a break from the computer screen, I go out on the deck and look up into the lush foliage of my backyard maple tree. How many times have I thanked my gentle Heavenly Shepherd for the gift of this tree? I have lost count.

A particular portion of scripture that has always intrigued me was when Jesus healed the blind man in Mark 8:

*"They came to Bethsaida, and some people brought a blind man
and begged Jesus to touch him. He took the blind man by the hand
and led him outside the village. When he had spit on the man's
eyes and put his hands on him, Jesus asked, 'Do you see anything?'
He looked up and said, 'I see people, they look like trees walking around.'
Once more Jesus put his hands on the man's eyes. Then his eyes were
opened, his sight was restored, and he saw everything clearly." Mark 8:22-25*

I am a lover of trees. I incorporate leaves and branches into silk ribbon designs on hats and quilts. I study the multi-colored greens and explosion of red, gold, and orange leaves through the seasons of nature. But throughout my journey with the love of nature so part of my being, I have never seen a face on the trunk of a tree.

What was so unique about this healing of the blind man? Why did Jesus pray for the healing of this blind man a second time? This story has always spoken in a powerful way to me personally. The Lord has spoken very clearly to me throughout my journey in how I view people. He does not want me to see humanity as a forest of trees but rather as unique individuals. To look beyond the surface of another and see down into the soul is the clear vision that I have sought for.

Throughout my years of teaching, regardless of the age of the student, I saw individuals. I looked into faces and saw their eyes. Sometimes I saw sorrow, at other times indifference. Delightfully, at times I saw joy and the desire to learn. But whatever expression I met as I taught, I wanted to see clearly. I always felt that when groups of people become as a forest and I could no longer see faces, it was time for me to retire from teaching.

While teaching at Fairlane, I enjoyed all my classes, but I think the "Child Development" course was the most fulfilling. I had learned early on the importance of not labeling students with preconceived information. I was a bit surprised when one particular student signed up for my class, as the reputation that followed this young man could give a teacher thoughts of concern. He was a tall, blond, strikingly handsome junior in high school.

On the first day of all my courses, I gave a brief review of class rules. One item was added to the list when it came to "Child Development." I would tell the students, "When you have completed this class, your life will be forever changed, as you will see young children with new eyes and appreciation."

I knew something was troubling this young man, as he was so disruptive in other classes.

On the first day of class, I took time to allow each student to express why they had enrolled in "Child Development." When it came time for this handsome blond gentleman, he explained he had a two-year-old sister he had a great deal of affection for.

He never acted out in my class. In fact, as the days slipped by, the hardness in his face softened. I would see tears in his eyes upon occasion. As he related the daily lessons of children to his own little sister, an expression of tender love replaced the defiant and rebellious countenance that had walked into my class on that first morning.

As I studied him, God's spirit spoke to me: "Tell him what you see." I went over and whispered that I wanted to see him out in the hall. I am sure he thought he was in trouble again.

We sat down on the step and the Shepherd of Heaven gave me words for that young man on a special day of his life. I told him I saw the tender heart under all those layers of pain, that I saw such promise in him, and that I prayed for him a great deal.

"You pray for me?" he exclaimed with surprise.

"Oh yes, and I have great faith in you!"

Years later, while living in Wyoming, I was visiting my family in Michigan for the holidays. My daughter Rachel was an associate pastor in the Ann Arbor area. It was a Sunday morning, and I was sitting with Craig and Sandy during the worship service. I felt a tap on my shoulder and looked around to see that very special student of so long ago with a big smile on his face, sitting with his friend, who had also been very special to me.

When there was a break, I met them both with a big bear hug. My handsome, blond young man turned to his friend and said, "See, I told you she believed in me."

He had heard I had come to Michigan for the holidays and had driven some distance to see if that teacher of many years past still believed in him.

I have to say that young man is still in my thoughts and prayers, and I do believe there is much goodness in that place down inside of him I saw so clearly in a classroom full of students.

This morning, I find myself, once again, excited and terrified at the same time. Will I ever advance past this complex set of emotions that are poles apart? Such is the life of the writer. Once, while attending a writing conference, I was listening very intently to the morning speaker, who had completed several very distinguished books. She asked a question: "Why do we write?" And then she answered the question: "We write because we must write. That voice within each of us will not be satisfied, until those thoughts are written on the page." How true has been that experience in my own life. Thoughts begin to surface, and then multiply until I have this driving force that pulls me upstairs to my computer, and then my mind goes blank. When this happens, I have to rely on that discipline and knowledge that the Great Shepherd of Heaven will come, and when I feel weak and inadequate, he will become my strength. A scripture that has been a source of faith for me in my own personal journey is found in II Corinthians:

> "My grace is sufficient for you, for my power is made perfect in weakness."
> II Corinthians 12:9

As I placed my hands upon the keyboard today, I looked up to see the picture of my grandson Luke, which was taken this last February when my family and I went back to see my mom.

I am so grateful when I look at Mitch and realize how much he loves my daughter and their two boys. He not only loves his family, but takes on the role of protector and makes family experiences special. He had taken the time to make out a list of each thing that would happen on Luke's first plane ride. When we were ready to depart from the Detroit airport, I looked across the aisle to see what the boys were doing.

Luke had put on a big set of plastic orange water goggles. I am not sure what the significance was to him, maybe a throwback to his children's collection of "Snoopy," but the goggles came on every time we were ready to begin another flight. Luke's choice of shoes during this season of his life is one blue shark and one green frog rubber boot.

The weekend passed all too quickly. We were packing up, getting ready to head back home, and Rachel wanted to take some pictures. Luke wanted Peeka (his name for Grandma) to see the dirt road he had discovered. It was a cold, blustery day with gray, troubled clouds. On went the multi-colored boots, coat, and mittens; Max was snuggled down in warm blankets in his stroller; and we were off. We went out to the north fields where the irrigation sprinkler was in sight. Luke began to walk down the deeply rutted path made by the huge tires that move in circular motion across the fields. Wayne had winterized the gigantic machine, and it sat out in the field, silent, waiting for spring. Mitch was navigating Max through the grass stubble, as we slowly made our way down to the old Alkali Creek, with its many memories of childhood.

I sit here today, once again studying this picture of one of my precious grandchildren. I remember how bravely Luke marched right into the northern winds, having a sense of place and family and confidence. He is only four years old, but when his Grandma Peeka is in Heaven, he will have stories penned to the page of his great-grandparents, Wallace and Edna Mae McClaflin, and their courage in facing life's challenges.

As I read through the stories penned on the pages of this manuscript, I am struck with the common, everyday memories I have related. Those circumstances and friendships that come along in one's life can aid in giving direction and purpose and make life a thing of value. I am amazed and pleased to see the book The Purpose-Driven Life in bookstores wherever I go. Rick Warren has captured the essence of what makes a life full of value and worth.

My brother Mike and his wife Linda have a busy life with all their travels to Africa. They both have a special place in the hearts of Craig, Shana, and Rachel. Upon occasion, they fly through Detroit International to see our family. When they come, I know they are weary from jet lag, but the schedule is hectic, as all of us want to spend time with them. One such trip, they were coming from Brussels, and the flight was delayed for hours, so they arrived very late at night. We had kept them up too late, but before each of us left for the evening, Mike called Reagan over to him. He took him up on his lap and said, "Young man, God has purposes for your life," and he prayed a blessing over him. That memory is indelibly printed on my heart and mind.

Uncle Mike McClaflin and namesake Reagan Michael Booher

As the stories of Teddy and Ronnie have unfolded throughout this manuscript, I am realizing what a special blessing they have been to me personally. I asked Teddy to share with you about the home tours for children she and Ronnie conducted for a number of years. I am sure they could fill several books with the personal stories of the children through the years, but I penned just a brief overview for you.

Lambing season on the Jones Farm and school tours

There was a glow on Teddy's face as she began to recount those days with the children.

"For me, it is so awesome to look at how God works in each and every one of our lives. God has used the sheep for Ronnie and me to be a way that we can share his love and bring to light how He cares for each and everyone. If you look at the lambs and the ewes through lambing season, when you go out into the sheep shed and see all the ewes bedded down, you just have a feeling of God's presence there. Unknown to Ronnie and

I, He has blessed us with the sheep, and part of our way to pass this blessing on has been through the field trips for the young people in our area. We had two purposes of having these field trips. One was to help young people to come back to the roots of the farm and see that you don't just go to the grocery store and buy everything."

"There is a certain amount of work that needs to be done and also the role that agriculture plays in the food chain. The way we got started with this was with LeGene Vaughn, who had a preschool. She always got so excited about the lambing season. She would bring the preschoolers, and the class usually had about fifteen children. This was before the time of kindergarten in our local schools. She would come out with the children and they would spend about an hour. First of all, what she wanted them to do was to have the joy and fun of feeding the orphan lambs, and that is the way it got started. Other teachers in the area heard about what was happening in the field trips from LeGene Vaughn. By word of mouth, we soon had teachers from Powell, Lovell, Cody, Wapita, and Clark School Districts calling to know if they could have a field trip out to the farm."

"Since our young people have been so far removed from agriculture, Ronnie and I felt it was very important to introduce them to the facts and correct information concerning livestock. So over the twenty years of tours we would have approximately between 400-450 young people from kindergarten through fifth graders each year. Mostly kindergarten and first graders would come. They would come and spend about two and a half to three hours, and we would take the young people through the process of feeding lambs. They would see how a baby lamb was born, which was always such an excitement for the young people. They would observe how the lamb was incased in the sack, the fluids, how the baby lamb was so wet and slimy to the touch, how the baby took its first breath, how it got the first suckle of milk, the colostrum that is so important, and how that baby started standing up."

"And of course we had chickens. They would see the eggs being laid by the hens and feel the warmth of the eggs. They would also have the opportunity to experience milking a goat, which was a new experience for many. Not only were we reaching the young people, many parents would come because they had never seen the birthing process. The children's eyes would just get big when they would see that little nose and little tongue come out for the first sign of birth. We especially had one little boy that got so excited that he got right down there beside Ronnie, and he was wanting to pull on that baby lamb. Ronnie let him help pull the lamb out, which we did with all the boys and girls. But he was just into the whole birthing process, and when he was done, the teacher handed him a napkin to wipe his hands off so he could participate in the feeding of the lambs and some other activities like the branding and numbering and this kind of thing, docking and castrating of the lambs. The teacher informed us that he took that napkin home and his mother had to put it in a scrapbook, and the last I knew it was still there."

"One other result of having the field trips is that we had one teacher who brought an autistic child, and she was very frightened of all the noises and all the smells and everything. We worked with that child and finally got her where she would touch a baby lamb and actually hold the bottle while a lamb was nursing, which was a tremendous breakthrough. Later on, the teacher reported back that the child had never spoken any words whatsoever, and after the experience out on the field trip to the lambing farm, she did speak a few words, so they felt that played an important role in the breakthrough for the child with autism."

"So you can see that God had His hand in many things even though, as we were doing the field trips, we did not really realize how God was working and how God was using the lambs and using us to help share what He had given us. It has always been a highlight in our lives. We still have young people which are out of school now, or some may be out of college in fact, come out and say we remember when we came out to see the lambing at your farm. I'll have mothers say, 'Are you the people that had the field trips?' So they are still recalling it as a wonderful experience, and it was all because of God. He has given us the sheep to share and to help see the joy and realize that humans are really no different than sheep. They need the love, they need the tender care, and they need the guidance, just like we do from our Heavenly Shepherd."

"One other side note is that these little children were so lovable, so adorable, and so innocent. We would be in the process of a ewe having a baby, and they would just really be watching and observing what was happening. We had one little girl whose eyes were just as big as saucers. We had this ewe pushing her baby lamb out, and she was in the cheering section on the side with those big, big beautiful eyes of hers, and she was saying to the ewe, 'Push, girl, push. Come on, girl, push.' Oh my goodness, when that baby came out, there was just all sorts of shouts of joy, and it was just such an exciting time to see how God has used all His creation to help us see Him."

"Preparing for the field trips was a challenge because we wanted to make sure that everything was just in order. We wanted the sheep shed to smell very good so that when the boys and girls would walk in, they wouldn't go, 'Ooh, ick.' We wanted a good odor. We didn't want a lot of manure so they would get it on their shoes. So it took quite a bit of work to keep the barn clean. We had to have everything covered with straw. If we had a lamb that died during the night, it would have to be taken care of. We did not want these young ones to see the dead lambs or anything like that. We started early in the morning, because we would have boys and girls arriving about nine o'clock, and they would be with us until a quarter to twelve. Through that time, we went into the shed and made sure that all the pens were strawed, watered, and fed. Where they came in, we would set down straw bales in a semicircle so they could see everything. And of course being there for a couple of hours, these little ones would get pretty hungry, so we always had cookies and some kind of a drink like hot chocolate or something prepared so that they could have refreshments."

"Many times, we would get thank-you notes back from the children, and I would think, 'Oh my goodness, what did we teach?' because it would be the cookies that they thought was the highlight of their trip that day. But as they grew older and as I would hear reports back from Mom and Dad, it was the lambing they remembered. This was such a wonderful opportunity because we had parents that would come with their children. We ran two classes a day, one in the morning and one in the afternoon. We would start the morning class about nine to about a quarter to twelve, and the second class, one to about a quarter to three. So that was sort of our schedule for the day, and many times we would have anywhere from ten children to fifty children per group."

"Usually, we would have about one parent for every four or five children, so we were also reaching a lot of the moms and dads, and they used this as an opportunity over the supper table to talk about a lot of things: about the birthing process, about caring for animals, and responsibilities. It just opened up the door for a lot of dialogue in families, which here again, God was working, even though I did not realize it. As I look back, I can see a lot of things that God had His hand in. Just helping us to get everything ready in time for all those kids and to give us the strength and energy was a blessing. As I said, we had about 450 boys and girls go through that lambing shed in those field trips each year, and we did it in approximately a two to three week period, and we did this for twenty years."

I knew of the tours to the Jones farm through the years, but until I sat across from Teddy that afternoon listening to her, I never realized before what dedication this farm couple had in giving so much to the young children of that community for so many years.

Throughout my personal story I have shared with you, I have spoken of that soft voice that many times comes with the wind. The message that comes is clear, and sometimes a great deal of faith and courage is needed to answer the call of God's spirit. And now you, the reader, might be asking, how could I possibly come to a place that I could hear this same Shepherd of Heaven? Actually, He is speaking to you all the time.

I wish that I could tell you life becomes easier, but it would be a lie. Through a process of living, we learn our lessons, and hopefully we learn them well. One important lesson of life for me is that I know I can trust the Heavenly Shepherd to do right by me. Time and again, I have found that the Lord does want to bless humanity with goodness and mercy spoken of in Psalm 23. I think of Corrie Ten Boom and Mother Theresa. Their lives were not of comfort and ease, as they had great struggles, and yet God's mercy and grace shone so brightly through their lives. I am sure in the many years of hard work and labor, Teddy and Ronnie did not realize that one day they would share with you and me the special Godly wisdom that has followed them throughout life.

You might be saying at this point, what do these stories have to do with me? I live in the city, and I have never even held a lamb. I will ask you to think for a moment. What are those dreams buried down in you? What purposes in life have been laid out for you that, if fulfilled, you would have a sense of great joy and worth? I will have to say, I have spent many late nights working on this manuscript. At times, I have felt a bit overwhelmed, but with all the discipline and work has come a joy so wonderful I can hardly contain it at times.

In living out that destiny God has for each of us, we not only have a sense of worth, but we can encourage another to walk in the paths of goodness and mercy.

> *"Praise be to the God and Father of our Lord Jesus Christ, the*
> *Father of compassion and the God of all comfort, who comforts*
> *us in all our troubles, so that we can comfort those in any trouble*
> *with the comfort we ourselves have received from God."*
> *II Corinthians 1:3 & 4*

CHAPTER 11:
AND I WILL DWELL IN THE HOUSE OF THE LORD FOREVER

I knew this day would come, and with it much excitement, as well as a bit of nervousness. Today is the day I will send my manuscript to the publisher. I have been promised that there will be technicians who will kindly walk me through the process of sending the entire manuscript in one document. Now for those grandchildren of mine, they say, "Oh Grandma that is so easy." But then they are of that younger generation, so bright and full of promise. My eldest grandson, Erik, who now towers over me, has blessed me time and again. He is one of those gifted in the area of computers. Many times he has come to patiently sit with me and teach me and show me what to do with this manuscript. I tell him I appreciate his help, but I don't know if he realizes the depth of appreciation I feel as the manuscript has been such a work of love. And then there is John who has always just been so special to me with an artist's eye that will be incorporated in many future stories.

Eldest grandsons, Erik and John Booher

There has to be closure to this book of stories of a shepherd girl from the windy northern plains of Wyoming. I could write volumes, but alas I have to include the last and final snippet of life's adventures on this juncture, as many other stories will follow this one. This morning, I turned to the well-known verses in Revelation:

> *"I am the Alpha and the Omega, the First and the Last, the*
> *Beginning and the End.*
> *Blessed are those who wash their robes, that they may have the*
> *right to the tree of life and may go through the gates into the city."*
> *Revelation 22:13-14*

As I have allowed myself time to reflect on those childhood experiences of walking with this Shepherd of Heaven, it is with a thankful heart I pen these final thoughts. One of my favorite stories in the Old Testament is of Caleb, going to spy out the Promised Land. It was a discouraged group of men who came back to meet with Moses. They saw the giants in the land they had been promised, and their hearts were full of fear. But then there was Caleb, who had another spirit. I am sure if you and

I would have the opportunity to follow this man on his journey of life, he had learned to know the voice of this Shepherd in the hard times, so that when he was faced with giants to conquer, Caleb knew God would be with him.

> *"But because my servant Caleb has a different spirit and follows me wholeheartedly, I will bring him into the land he went to, and his descendants will inherit it."*
> *Numbers 14:24*

During my time of working with UW Cooperative Extension, the highlights of those years were the times Teddy and I worked together. We both had an innate love for children, and people in general, so we drew energy from each other. One of the programs that comes to mind dealt with anger management. After presenting the program a number of times, we pulled together the resource materials that most related to audiences, and then we settled on a name: "Tiger in Your Tank." One particular three-week session we taught was with a group of high-risk young people from the ages of ten to sixteen. It was not an easy assignment, but we worked together to reassure these youngsters. After the last session, we spent a few minutes allowing the participants to give us some feedback. One sixteen-year-old gentleman raised his hand. "After taking this class, I believe I am going to be able to take control of my raging temper, and I think I will be able to have a life now." A hush fell over the group, as each person in that room knew the courage it took for that young man to be so honest. When the room was put back in order, and the lights were turned out, Teddy and I went out to the parking lot and said good-bye. We both felt an incredible peace, knowing young people had walked away from those sessions with a hope for the future.

I acquired many excellent resources along the way on resiliency. I am so grateful that I had the privilege of working with Dr. Ben Silliman, UW Family Life Specialist, as he was very instrumental in introducing me to many resources on resiliency that have enriched my life and I have applied to many programs.

I attended a seminar on "Hurting Children," with Ruth Arent, M.A., M.S.W. She had done extensive work with hurting children. Fortunately, I brought home a resource manual, Trust Building with Children Who

<u>Hurt</u>. It was chucked full of materials I would use in the coming years. One particular resource came from years of documented research for the difference between "Children Who Hurt" and "Children Who Hate" (Arent, page 2).

Because Teddy and I worked mostly in a secular setting, we knew we needed to use wisdom. But when it was time for me to relate to the issue of hurt versus hate, Teddy would step back and let me take all the time needed. I would look into the faces of those in the audiences, and I would feel such deep compassion for them. I would tell them I didn't want to offend anyone, but one of the greatest gifts I had found in life was knowing that God would give me the ability to forgive. I could come through any storm, because I knew regardless of how weak I felt, or how angry, I could count on the Great Shepherd of Heaven to come and fill my heart with love, so that I could go on in life's journey and have peace and hope for a future and be filled with mercy and grace all the days of my life.

We conducted many seminars together, with all kinds of groups and settings of people. This was a poem I had penned during that time of working which we used to bring a closure to the programs we conducted:

CHOICES

The longer I walk through this journey of life,
I realize the power I possess within to make choices,
Choices daily, Sometimes minute by minute.
Great personal courage and faith at times are necessary,
When I make choices where there are sacrifices,
When I choose love over hate,
When I choose forgiveness over holding on to bitterness,
When I choose to look beyond myself
To see that one who needs my caring.
Yes, life is a choice.
So soon my days will pass.
What will I leave behind?
Dear God, give me the courage to choose goodness.

Patricia, October 22, 1996

Life is full of choices that come with each day; sometimes they come moment by moment, but God is mindful of our cry, when we need that added boost of courage. I am sure the reason I have always had such a deep love for children is because I have been very aware from childhood that knowing this Shepherd so early in life was a great privilege.

When I hear of a young person committing suicide, it always brings grief to my soul. What a sense of loss it is to know they will never have the opportunity to soar with eagle's wings or see a little robin red breast with a wounded wing fly off into the morning sunlight. I never have believed in the generation gap because it is not in the season of life we find ourselves that makes the difference, it is that innate ability to look beyond ourselves and to truly love that other person regardless of age, rank, or serial number. There is something so special when we find that person who just loves us unconditionally, who stands in the wings and cheers us on, who has the time to listen, who reassures us regardless of circumstance that we have a future and a hope.

Wyoming Shepherd, Ronnie Jones holding triplet, Sammy

I wanted to share with you, the reader, this testimony given by Ronnie of his own personal walk with God. It is so filled with truth, honesty, and tenderness.

"Sheep have played a big role throughout my life. They are a rewarding animal. They will try to stay away but they still have trust in you, especially as they get to know you better. As I think about my life, I have been like the sheep, as I knew the Lord early on when I was young but then I worked for my own self, thinking I could do my own thing, and so consequently drifted away from the Lord, just like the sheep might stray from the shepherd. I never got into a lot of trouble but I could have. Of course, sheep are the same way, as they drift away and move into a hollow away from the shepherd in search of food and maybe a better pasture that appears to be greener. When I looked at myself as a human, I probably thought the same thing. And then as I think about coming back closer to the Lord, I realize the safety and self-assurance the Lord gives me. I'm kind of like Moses; I drifted around for about forty years where I didn't really keep the Lord completely away, and I often thought of the Lord but I wasn't actively engaged with Him."

"I came to a time I wished to know the Lord more closely, so for about the last ten years I have come to know Him more deeply. I watched my wife Teddy, who was coming to know the Lord more closely, even before myself. She wanted me to also enjoy that presence of the Lord. We became closer to the Lord through a program in a local church in which we became involved. As we participated in the Bible teaching program, we also became closer to the Lord, and I feel that I found the Lord Jesus and gave my soul over to Him. As I continue my life, I find a lot of peace and comfort in knowing the Lord and knowing that He is my personal savior and that I will be able to be with Him at my life's end. I find comfort in this, knowing that God has given me that grace and the chance that I will be with Him forever throughout eternity."

As I reached over and turned off the tape recorder, it was quiet in that kitchen, as I realized I had just heard the heartfelt words of a kindly shepherd man who had come full circle, and life had taken on a depth and purpose as the Great Shepherd of Heaven had come into a clear focus in Ronnie Jones.

I have often referred to the work done by Erik Erikson in relation to the eight stages of life. In the eighth and final stage of life, "Integrity versus Despair," I have penned a quote that parallels what we are relating in reference to living with purpose: "Only in him who in some way has taken care of things and people and has adapted himself to the triumphs and disappointment adherent to being, the originator of others or the generator of products and ideas—only in him may gradually ripen the fruit of these seven stages." (Erikson, page 269)

I have known individuals who have lived their last days on this earth in great despair. At times, I have been asked to attend a person's funeral, so that there would be someone sitting in the audience. And then I have attended funerals where there was great sadness, as the individual had given such an investment to others that their passing on to be in Heaven would leave a great vacancy. They had completed this journey of life with great integrity. In other words, they had left a rich inheritance to those they loved.

As I again look at the picture of my grandson heading into the wind, walking in the deeply furrowed path on the old homestead where I had my roots, my prayer is that my life has planted many seeds of righteousness for future generations of humanity.

> *"Now I commit you to God and to the word of his grace, which can build you up and give you an inheritance among all those who are sanctified." Acts 20:32*

As we come to know this Shepherd of Heaven, we gain an assurance that He is like that rock I would sit on in the late summer days in Shell Canyon. He is not moved or shaken by the affairs of man, but looks with great compassion on each of us.

The Lord has promised that He will never leave us nor forsake us, and the Bible tells you and me that if we accept Him, when our life is ended we will be with Him forever and forever and forever:

> *"Do not let your hearts be troubled. Trust in God; trust also in me. In my Father's house are many rooms; if it were not so, I would have told you. I am going there to prepare a place for you.*

> *And if I go and prepare a place for you, I will come back and take you to be with me that you also may be where I am." John 14:1–3*

> *"But our citizenship is in Heaven. And we eagerly await a Savior from there, the Lord Jesus Christ, who, by the power that enables him to bring everything under his control, will transform our lowly bodies so that they will be like his glorious body." Philippians 3:20*

When I first began to write those first poems on that winter day looking out on the Big Horn Mountain range, with heavy snow coming down, and my faithful little dog sleeping beside my chair, courage was required to pen the first words. And then rapidly the words came with one poem after another. And so, my friend, I have shared with you some of my sorrows, but more than that, stories of a rich inheritance filled with much joy and peace, given to me from my family and friends, and most of all from the Heavenly Shepherd, who is so dear to my heart. I must now bring closure to this part of many more stories that will follow, and so I will go to that quiet place where poems come to mind.

PASSAGE

You there standing by the sidelines,
Thinking your time has passed you by,

The comfort of a warm room setting next to the fire brings solace,
But only for a short time.
Those questions on your mind, What if? What if?

Though your gray hair is now turning to shades of glistening white,
Can you not go back and remember your stories of life for the young ones?

Don't pass them off as the reckless generation for they have great promise.
They have many challenges before them.
Your smile of encouragement will give them wings to fly.

Just as the eagle taking
flight in the blustery clouds of northern skies,
Or a precious grandchild heading into the wind in a deep rut of soil
From many years of life's experience
You have choices that can make an impact long after you are asleep.

Will you give hope and integrity, or will your message be one of despair?
The Great Shepherd of Heaven calls you now,
To that quiet place where He will give you wisdom of rare beauty
That you can pass on to the young ones.

Not everyone has been given the privilege of coming
Into this season of life.
Many others died young on a battlefield far from home.
Some were taken early from the ravages of cancer,
But you dear friend can pass on a rich heritage,

So get up now and be about the task of living.
Take the hand of a young child.
Bless life and all its goodness.
But most of all
Be thankful.
Patricia, December 2008

Grandson, Luke Ross walking in north pasture on McClaflin homestead, Powell, Wyoming, picture donated by his mother, Rachel Ross

REFERENCES

Bible Translations:

Life Application Study Bible. New International Version, Tyndale House and Zondervan, 1991.

The Thompson Chain-Reference Study Bible. New King James Version, B.B. Kirkbride Bible Co. Indianapolis, Indiana, 1983.

Resource Books

Arent, Ruth P. Trust Building with Children Who Hurt. The Center for Applied Research in Education, West Nyack, New York, 1992.

Curran, Dolores. Traits of a Healthy Family. Ballantine, New York, 1983.

Erikson, Erik. Childhood and Society. W.W. Norton, New York, 1963.

Stoltz, Paul, Adversity Quotient, Turning Obstacles into Opportunities. John Wiley and Sons, New York, 1997.

Kubler-Ross, Elisabeth and David Kessler. On Grief and Grieving: Finding the Meaning of Grief through the Five Stages of Loss. Scribner, New York, 2005.

Warren, Rick. The Purpose-Driven Life. Zondervan, Grand Rapids, Michigan, 2002.

Woolen, Steven, M.D. and Sybil Wolin, Ph.D. The Resilient Self, How Survivors of Troubled Families Rise Above Adversity. Villard, New York, 1994.

Songs:

"In the Garden." Lydia Baxter (1809–1874) and William H. Doane (1832–1915). Gospel Publishing House, Springfield, Missouri, 1969.

"It is Well with My Soul." Horatio G. Spafford (1828–1888) and Philip P. Bliss (1838–1876). Gospel Publishing House, Springfield, Missouri, 1969.

"There is a Balm in Gilead. A version of the refrain can be found in Washington Glass's 1854 hymn "The Sinner's Cure."

Upcoming Story

"HERE, LAMBY, LAMBY, LAMBY"

As each of us walk through this journey of life, we think we know how that path will lead and then along the way, sometimes we find ourselves diverging onto another road. This is one of those times with me, and what a great adventure this has been.

When this project first began, it was early in January and I was planning on writing a children's curriculum for our mission team who would be traveling to Kenya, East Africa, in the summer. I had chosen the 23rd Psalm, which for many reasons is very close to my heart. In just a matter of a few weeks, I realized I had been away from the lambing sheds for too many years, and I needed to refresh my knowledge of caring for orphan lambs.

I booked a flight to Wyoming to spend a few days on the old homestead with Mom and visit childhood friends, Teddy and Ronnie Jones, who still have flocks of sheep. I took a friend along, Virla Harrell, who is a watercolor artist. She had helped me with the transcripts of interviews with homesteaders for the other manuscript that needed completion.

By the time I could leave my work and travel to Wyoming, the lambing season was almost over. I didn't know if there would be any newborn lambs for us to see. As we drove up to the farmhouse, Teddy met us with a smile on her face with news that a Suffolk ewe had given birth to triplets early that morning. There were two other orphan lambs Teddy was caring for in the farmhouse that would become the two main characters of the children's story.

Virla painted a watercolor picture of Ronnie holding one of the triplets we named Sammy. This picture would make its way to Africa with the 23rd Psalm written in English and Swahili in an overlay.

When I returned home and began working once again on the curriculum, it soon became apparent to me that a new novel was formulating in my mind and my heart and down in the soul of me. I struggled with this for a few days, because there was another manuscript just waiting completion in my upstairs office. After many nights of waking up way before the first signs of morning, the stories would come to me with such intensity, I had to give in and begin writing them down.

Bum lambs, Bo and Susie in children's book

The story of the triplets and the two wounded lambs we named Bo and Susie would have to become a children's story. This is actually a true story of little lambs that had been wounded and were fortunate to have been born on the Jones farm. The interviews taken from transcripts from conversations with Teddy and Ronnie about their lifelong vocation of caring for sheep and their love of the 23rd Psalm weaves a beautiful story relating to two wounded lambs. The title of the children's story comes from the way Teddy would call her orphan lambs to her out in the barnyard at feeding time: "Here, lamby, lamby, lamby."

Day after day as I would write the story, I would see before me faces of little African children in the worst of situations. We were going to an area where the death rate from disease was high, and many children were left as orphans. Each week I would take the chapter I had written and share it with the children at church. We all grew to love these three little lambs.

One day when I called to check on the three little lambs, Teddy had to tell me Bo died. When I got off the phone, I couldn't understand why I felt such sadness over an orphan lambing dying. That week as I read the next chapter of the lamby story to the children, we all cried. I wondered how I would be able to write about Bo dying, but the Great Shepherd of Heaven would impress on my heart that I was going to a faraway place where death was an everyday occurrence. He wanted to reassure those little children that He loved them.

Grandma Patty with mission team in Kenya, East Africa, picture donated by Dan Ross Photographs

And so we traveled to Africa and shared with the beautiful children there the story of the 23ʳᵈ Psalm and of Sammy, Bo and Susie. There were throngs of children and even now as I write, their faces are imprinted on my mind and spirit.

Each evening we would have the children make a line and we would pass out the little picture of the Wyoming shepherd holding Sammy with an inscription of the 23ʳᵈ Psalm overlaid to stay with each of them, long after the mission team had returned home.

And so here is the story of a triplet named Sammy, who narrates the story of two little orphan lambs who became great friends. After the death of Bo, Susie missed him terribly, but soon she was taken back to the sheep sheds, where she looked for other little orphan lambs that needed her care. This is a story of inspiration, a story of friendship, and a story of courage and forgiveness.

Printed in the United States
141540LV00001B/2/P